Also by Lyn Lifshin

Why Is the House Dissolving?
   (1969)

Lady Lyn (1970)

Leaves and Night Things (1970)

Moving by Touch (1971)

Black Apples (1971, 1973)

40 Days, Apple Nights (1972)

Museum (1973)

Plymouth Women (1974)

Old House Poems (1975)

Upstate Madonna (1975)

Paper Apples (1975)

North (1976)

Shaker House Poems (1976)

Glass (1978)

Leaning South (1978)

Offered by Owner (1978)

Sunday Poems (1979)

Blue Dust New Mexico (1982)

Madonna Who Shifts for Herself
   (1983)

Naked Charm (1984, 1990)

Kiss the Skin Off (1985)

*The Camping Madonna at Indian
   Lake* (1986)

Raw Opals (1987)

Red Hair and the Jesuit (1988)

Skin Divers (1989)

Not Made of Glass (1990)

On the Outside (1990)

The Doctor Poems (1991)

The Innocents (1991)

Reading Lips (1991)

Marilyn Monroe (1994)

*Shooting Kodachromes in the
   Dark* (1994)

Parade (1995)

Color and Light (1995)

Blue Tattoo (1995)

*Cold Comfort: Selected Poems
   1970–1996* (1997)

Before It's Light (1999)

*A New Film About a Woman In
   Love with the Dead* (2002)

When a Cat Dies (2004)

Another Woman's Story (2004)

Barbie Poems, vols. 1 & 2
   (2004)

*She Was Found Treading Water
   Deep Out in the Ocean* (2005)

The Daughter I Don't Have
   (2005)

*The Licorice Daughter: My Year
   with Ruffian* (2006)

In Mirrors (2006)

A Black Sparrow Book
David R. Godine · Publisher
Boston

poems by
Lyn Lifshin

ANOTHER WOMAN WHO LOOKS LIKE ME

This is
A Black Sparrow Book
published in 2006 by
David R. Godine, Publisher
Post Office Box 450
Jaffrey, New Hampshire 03452
www.blacksparrowbooks.com

Some of these poems were published, sometimes in different versions, in the following
periodicals: *ACM (Another Chicago Magazine), Apple, Aurean, Baltimore Review,
Borderlands, Canadian Women, Carolina Quarterly, Centennial Review, Chiron, The
Christian Science Monitor, Colorado North Review, Concrete Wolf, Connecticut Poetry
Review, Connecticut Review, Epoch, 5 AM, Footwork, Free Lunch, Frontiers, Greensboro
Review, Gulf Stream, Hampton-Sydney Poetry Review, Harpur Palato, Heaven Bone,
Heeltap, Hollins Critic, Hunger, Images, Impetus, The International Poetry Review,
Jabberwock Review, Kaimana: Literary Arts, The Ledge, Lilliput Review, Lips, The Little
Magazine, Lullwater Review, Main Street Rag, Many Mountains Moving, Michigan
Quarterly, The Mid-American Poetry Review, Milkweed Chronicle, Minnesota Review,
New Delta Review, The New Laurel Review, New Letters, New York Quarterly,
Northwest Review, On the Bus, The Paterson Literary Review, Phoebe, Plastic Tower,
Poetry Depth, Rainbow Review, Rattle, Razor Wire, Room of One's Own, Seneen Review,
So to Speak, Sojourner, South Ash Press, South Carolina Quarterly, Southern Indiana
Review, Sou'wester, Sulphur River, The Sun, Synchronicity, Texas Review, 13th Moon, 360
Degrees, Thunder Sandwich, Tule Review, Wascana Review, Waterways, Whitefish,* and
William and Mary Review.

Photograph of Lyn Lifshin copyright © Scogin Mayo
The Black Sparrow Books pressmark is by Julian Waters
www.waterslettering.com

Library of Congress Cataloging-in-Publication Data
Lifshin, Lyn.
Another woman who looks like me : poems / by Lyn Lifshin — 1st ed.
    p. cm.
"A Black Sparrow Book"
ISBN 13 : 9781-57423-198-4 (pbk. : alk. paper)
ISBN 10 : 1-57423-198-7 (pbk. : alk. paper)
PS3562.I4537 A83   2006
811.54—dc22
2005036557

First Edition
Printed in Canada

contents

slippery blisses

Champlain, Branbury, the lakes at night   13
Lake Champlain   14
First day of school   15
Going to the Catholic school   16
Some winters Champlain froze   18
Lying out in the fields where there'd be
   wild strawberries   19
Some afternoons when nobody was fighting   20
Nights it was too hot to stay in the apartment   21
September 28, 1999   22
My mother makes me into a Spanish dancer   23
Hardly anyone in my family could sew   25
Past the abandoned railroad   27
Saturday movies   28
In front of my mother's vanity   30
Lips   32
Tongue   34
Eyes   36
The jewelry box, the room of lavender and dripping   38
In Middlebury, the bee man dies   40
The bee man's first nights in earth   41

a love of blueness

In front of my mother's vanity   42
There should be as many words for loneliness   44
Though mice have gnawed the green candles   45
After the house of ghosts   48
Blue Tuesday blues   49
Tuesday blue   50
After not writing much for three months   51

Fingers 52

A woman goes into the mall 53

Metro, January 8 55

Another woman who looks like me 57

I wear my hair long 59

written on the body of night

Venice Daphne run backwards 60

E-mail message 62

Black sweater in May 63

The apple orchard man 65

The first time 66

From the mattress on the floor under
the flaming sky photo 67

Dream of smoke and orchids . . . 68

The man who brought emerald mandarin oranges 70

Rescued again 71

The man who says floating blonds come thru his eyes 73

It was better, he said 74

"The wholesale artificial limbs business," she says . . . 75

Expulsion from the garden 76

Two Thursdays 77

Lemon sun, Saturday 78

Rich dark 79

That February 80

Blue Sunday 81

Those nights 82

Dialing your number 83

This time I can leave you 85

A woman went into the cemetery 86

Everything I have you don't have 87

I never wanted you 88

Now you've spent a whole month in the ground 89

I read in a clip that your son said you'd have liked 90

White trees in the distance 91

"Kiss, Baby," the new film 92

Like the woman wild to have calligraphy 94

When I read about another woman whose pleasure came 95

Moving by touch 96

The origin of the seasons according to the Delawares 99

When they wheeled you away 100

When he said you never write

       any good poems about me 101

When I think of him leaving 102

parallel worlds

I think of my grandfather 103

If my grandmother could have written

       a postcard to Odessa 104

From the first weeks in New York . . . 105

May 10 106

The other fathers 107

Like some lies we tell ourselves 108

Wooden medicine cabinet 109

My father's wallet 110

The cousins' party 111

Vacation 112

My sister's birthday 114

She was two when she locked the bathroom door

       behind her 116

My sister's film 118

Images of my cousin 119

September 23, 1996   120

Hearing my cousin   121

If you read her life backwards in dripping lilacs   122

Photographs in my mother's pocketbook   123

The blue candy dish   124

My uncle sells the store   126

Not half as much but double   128

My uncle is dead   129

The past is melting in my fingers   130

from another world

A week after my mother's real birthday   132

Cows, dolls, and babies float in my mother's head . . .   133

She was Frieda Lazarowitz   135

the days between

June 30, 1938, record cold   137

The night before I was born   139

July 12 birthday poem   140

On the fifth anniversary of the night she eloped   141

The bottle of teeth   142

"Vamoose," I hear a 30s or 40s torch singer belt out   143

In Rexall's, Middlebury   144

The blue violin candy dish   145

interlude

My mother in front of the powder-flecked vanity   147

My mother's knife   148

Tho my mother said she forgot how to make
    hospital corners   150

I think of my mother on the blue couch   152

My mother begs me to wait with her in the dark   154
My mother, who could always see a smudge of grit . . .   155
My mother's tub   156
There's nobody   157
The leaves cold, thick   159
After my mother goes   160

flickering light

My mother's last trip on her own to Grand Union   161
That April   163
My mother used to rub my back   164
My mother, just looking out at me   165
Red sky at morning   166
Your mother has too much fight to be
        anywhere near death   167
That last afternoon my mother wanted
        bread and butter in milk   168
My mother wants buttered bread in milk   169
Strange pocketbooks scattered thru the house   171

returning in autumn

"You must have had an actress in the family"   172
It was all comedy and tragedy   174
Hearing "Bloomsday" as "Blues Day"   175
Like a woman of ancient China   176
While I was looking for photographs   177
The emptiness, Nancy says   178
Seeing the mother and daughter laughing
        over coffee in Macy's   179
Even after 9 years   180
After the IV, after the Demerol and Compazine   181

Three days before my mother's real birthday   183
May 28th, what would have been
        my mother's 90th birthday   185

things behind the sun

The wallpaper in my mother's hall   186
Feet   188
The gold dress   189
Wintergreen   191
In my mother's wooden medicine cabinet   192
The guava and turquoise bath mat   193
The red sweater   194
My mother's nicotine-stained clock   196
The mourning ribbons in boxes of jewelry   197

darkness in the light

September 26, 1996   198
Mid November   199
Late November   200
Just after forsythia, after icy rain   201
When spring melts the ground   202
Days the dead are too loud   204
Overnight the trees   205
March 20, 2000   206
April   208
Some afternoons   209
Suddenly by the first of April, the palest rose
        wrapped tight   210
In the park, before ballet   211
Quiet morning, August   212
Cherry blossoms in darkness   213
Downstairs, the dark studded   214

the wind won't carry us

The swans must be here   215

Heron on ice   216

Dead goose the leaves drift over   217

Dead goose under burnt orange leaves   218

The mourning doves   219

Swan-free, that's our goal, the warden says   221

☐ slippery blisses

Champlain, Branbury, the lakes at night

always women in the
dark on porches talking
as if in blackness their
secrets would be safe.
Cigarettes glowed like
Indian paintbrush.
Water slapped the
deck. Night flowers
full of things with wings.
Something you could
almost feel like the fingers
of a boy moving, as if
by accident, under
sheer nylon and cotton
in the dark movie house
as the chase gets louder,
there and not there,
something miscarried
that maybe never was.
The mothers whispered
about a knife, blood.
Then, they were laughing
the way you sail out of
a dark movie theater
into wild light as if no
thing that happened
happened

Lake Champlain

We could hear Louis Armstrong
if the wind blew right.
On our side of the lake,
we listened to the baby-

sitter's stories
of what they did to children
in Germany in the tunnels,
my mother's cigarette a

firefly on the porch across
the dark jade grass, a
night-light. I imagined
hair straight as that of

the girl at the rink with
one green eye, one blue,
her gaze as hypnotic
as the stories of what

people could do. I
didn't know what
might uncoil in the night.
Or that, though I felt

I was storing up sun,
catching light like
minnows, in the fall
ahead there wouldn't
be one night I didn't

wake up screaming
in dreams of fire

First day of school

My mother in the doorway
getting smaller as she would,
a kite burning my palm
as the wind jolts it from
me, a thud in my belly
that even at six wasn't
flat as I'd like it to be.
Mrs. Butterfield, a ship
that could take me where
my mother wouldn't go,
steaming closer as if she
could block what I was
leaving behind, my mother
in a worn coat already
counting the hours

Going to the Catholic school

once a year, bundled in wool
pea coats and snow pants,
mufflers dotted with ice crystals
tightly around our faces so the
incense we were sure would be
too thick to breathe in wouldn't
make us sneeze. Under our
snow pants, soft corduroy jeans;
over our gloves, our thickest
mittens: we had heard about
rulers smashing bones and skin,
that patent-leather shoes were
forbidden. Something about the
stained-glass light on the pale
nuns with enormous crosses
and rosaries kept us huddled and
close, walking with only side-
long glances at the Jesus with
bleeding chest, as scary as *The
Thing* where Jessica, whose
father was a minister, shrieked
when the blob filled the screen.
We didn't know why the Catholic
girls couldn't come to our school
but would come later, in high
school. Or why everything
had a smell we never smelled
anywhere else, or how we'd ever
catch up in Latin when we had to.
The dark-haired girls with
their dangling faces of Mary
they kissed before a ball game

or a test seemed as exotic
as what was hidden under their
white confirmation dresses,
flesh we heard would later writhe
and twist and do the wild thing
since it would be ok once
they confessed

Some winters Champlain froze

always with places
where the ice was
too soft to hold the
cars that flaunted
their metal. Otter
Falls grew thick
crusty beards of ice.
St Mary's against
the salmon sky.
Walking over the
bridge was freezing.
I wanted stories of
my father in a cold
hut in Russia without
a radio like ours, only
wind and the chickens.
I wanted a story of
sleeping in straw
with horses' breath
for a fire, of silver
moon, black pines

Lying out in the fields where there'd be wild strawberries

only strawberry leaves
that March afternoon,
the sun a glow we
hardly saw the months
of snow. We lay on
our backs. No, I told
my mother later,
the ground was dry.
Birds all around,
dandelions we opened
already the palest
color of sun. My green
parka on the pale
green hill, our eyes
closed, smelling
the smell of things
growing: hair, summer,
and tho by mid afternoon
we'd shiver in the shade,
our skin stayed pink,
sun-kissed this early

Some afternoons when nobody was fighting

my mother took out
walnuts and chocolate
chips. My sister and
I plunged our fingers
in flour and butter
smoother than clay.
Pale dough oozing
between our fingers
while the house filled
with blond bars rising.
Mother in her pink dress
with black ballerinas
circling its bottom
turned on the Victrola,
tucked her dress up into
pink nylon bloomer pants,
kicked her legs up in the
air and my sister and I
pranced thru the living
room, a bracelet around
her. She was our Pied
Piper and we were
the children of Hamelin,
circling her as close as the
dancers on her hem

Nights it was too hot to stay in the apartment

we drove to the lake, then stopped
at my grandmother's. The grownups
sat in the screened porch on wicker
or the glider, whispering above the
clink of ice in wet glass. Spirea and
yellow roses circled the earth under
stars. A silver apple moon. Bored
and still sweaty, my sister and I
wanted to sleep out on the lawn
and dragged out our uncle's army
blankets and chairs for a tent. We
wanted the stars on our skin, the
small green apples to hang over
the blanket to protect us from bats.
From the straw mats, peonies glowed
like planets, and if there was a breeze,
it was roses and sweat. I wanted
our white cats under the olive green
with us, their tongues snapping up
moths and whatever buzzed thru the
clover. For an hour the porch
seemed miles away as we grew itchy
with bug bites and felt our shirts fill
with night air, our hair grow curlier.
Then Mother came to fold up the blankets
and chairs and I wished I was old
enough to stay alone until dawn or
small enough to be scooped up, asleep
in arms that would carry me up the
still hot apartment stairs and into
sheets I wouldn't know were
still warm until morning

September 28, 1999

I think of walking
home on Main Street,
the smoke of burning
leaves. Past Otter Creek,
apricot light on window
panes. Pumpkins on
stairs already. I could
smell the leaves in my
hair, itchy wool on
bare legs I wished were
thinner. I wanted to
be lifted out of my
plump body and given
a tall skinny one.
I could smell apples,
the wind over the falls
curling hair my mother
always said was
full of gold, special
as she said I was to her,
so much she said I
couldn't see in me
but would later

My mother makes me into a Spanish dancer

Halloween on Main Street. For weeks that October I pose
in a colorless cotton dress she will dye to flame and
burning maple. My belly's round under the long torso
she will pin and cut. I stand in front of the Heywood-
Wakefield vanity while Otter Falls crashes near the window
and wish I was as skinny as Vivian and Regina. I don't see my
thick curly hair as anything but full of snarls; I long for
straight slim blond braids. My mother is sure I am a beauty,
molds cloth to camouflage baby fat she promises I'll outgrow.
Somewhere in the talcum powder she hunts the tortoiseshell
comb for the mantilla. I shift from one ugly brown shoe to
the other as she mumbles thru pins to stand still. My
mother, who rarely sews, is transforming the colorless
into what throbs with red, a blood staccato. Later she'll paint
a beauty mark on my cheek as if to stamp what I'll become
out there for everyone. My mother, who wanted to dance—
who danced on her toes barefoot against her father's wishes,
when he wasn't looking—brings out castanets and clacks
them over her head behind me in the mirror, her legs
that will stay lovely into her 70s kicking high, her body
moving more easily than mine will in the blood-colored
dress I'm sure I will trip on parading thru Main St, one hand
clutching the Spanish comb, another gripped to keep from
falling. I will never love red, even when I dye my hair
blond, put on *Love That Red* lipstick, but will prefer subtle
shades, faded blues and mauves, dust rose and violet.
Even when my life seems to go exactly as I'd choose, I won't
have my mother's fire—what they called in her yearbook "joie de
vivre"—her dancing black eyes daring any man to drive to
Boston or New York City and back for a cup of coffee or
dancing on the ferry all night and dashing off to sell the most
books in Macy's. I'll keep the dress in a drawer long after it

clings a little too tightly over my belly, but when I clean out
my mother's house years later I will be too drained to rescue it.
But I'll always dream of her hands and gloves tinted with red dye,
think how she always went for the most vivid colors, wild purples,
emerald green, bright royal blue, and in her last October,
a red wool coat I now keep in my closet. I forget to wear it,
wrap myself in black velvet, muted fleece. When I stand
before it looking for ballet tights, I think of the red dress
swirling, the bottom flirtatious, free, and of how my
mother, even in her last weeks, never chose the blond
pale tapioca pudding, the colorless custards cancer
patients are supposed to crave, but instead wanted
something she could put her teeth in, rare roast beef
or lamb or steaks, dripping ruby and garnet blood

Hardly anyone in my family could sew

except my father, who shortened pants customers
bought at Lazarus Dept Store noontimes, even
after he started with white pills under his tongue,
who trudged up the apartment stairs, green baggy pants
for Robert Frost to wear while wandering thru Main St.
My mother once made me a Spanish dancer's
costume but I don't remember her sewing anything
else. I tried to sew a hem on a skirt for a Christmas
pageant that unraveled, like so much would, on
stage. For Girl Scouts, 20 of us had little squares
to sew into a patch work quilt. I preferred painting,
working on science projects with huge papier-mâché
models of the eye I filled with Vaseline and clear
glue. Or writing poems about the apple blossoms,
how dark moved in and I could almost smell it.
Sewing, like cooking, had too many rules. One aunt
tried to teach me to knit but I dropped stitches, as awkward
as someone playing piano in padded gloves thick enough
for 50 below freezing. I no longer remember who made
the two afghans—blue for my mother, a rainbow one for
Nanny—but it wasn't my mother. If a button broke, a
blouse would stay that way as if there never was time for
anything small or painstaking. I sewed the way I wrap a
gift: as if I'd slapped paper and tape together, running from
a burning room. You can see this today if you check out
my ballet slippers. There was no Singer machine, no small-
girl toy version. My mother's button box just grew heavier.
None of us were good at following patterns. When I tried
to trace a tiny bathroom rug on a new square of pile, even
that was a disaster. Some think of sewing as relaxing as
yoga, almost like playing music, creative as cooking (some
thing else few in my family thrilled to). I love the sheen of

velvet, satin, taffeta, the nub of fleece and fur and how
light ripples over the thick wine and onyx fibers, and I can
imagine a room of women stitching and weaving, gossiping
and sewing, but could never see myself in those rooms

Past the abandoned railroad

where boys tried to lean
into a nipple if you walked
thru the thick wet leaves
of Frog Alley where tourists
sip cappuccino on the wrought-
iron chairs. When, finally,
some boy asked me to dance
he tried to put his tongue
in deep, his fingers past my blue
dress dotted with rhinestones,
near where we bowled on New
Year's Eve, and Sylvia, the tall
elegant woman, told me later
I had lovely skin. From the
bridge at Otter Creek, the old
marble mill grew rivulets
of ice, like bars, as if to cage
the cold, the frozen spiders.
Someone buried marbles
ground to dust past the college
spires, the last thing the girl
with a baby growing in
her saw flashing by as she
jumped into the whirlpool's
icy logs. Some nights I
was sure I could hear her
moaning as the falls crashed,
spit ice up to Main Street
and I ran, as if the crush of
cold froth was a lure

Saturday movies

Before movies with boys
trying to put their hands in
under angora or a felt
jumper and after the
endless westerns, dust,
hats and hooves pounding,
boring we thought, sucking
on Junior Mints, it was
the movies with stars
we ached to be. Vera-Ellen
with a 16-inch waist,
Pier Angeli (pale and shy,
Photoplay said) in a
peasant dress I cut out and
put on my wall near
the cinch-belted Vera,
stood near my mother's
mirror with my waist pulled
in, sucking myself into
myself as if I could
swallow my pink glasses,
little paunch. I never wanted
to be Marilyn Monroe,
Jane Russell or Jayne
Mansfield, women with huge
hips, breasts, but Audrey
Hepburn—slim, able to slip in
to a new life, escape from
my grandfather sneakily
lurking behind me at
parties or the movies. I
wanted to wear postage-size

cashmere, pale and silvery
shoes I could balance
forever in, suspended on
toes that could brush your
skin while you slept,
hover around your quilt, a
movie-queen angel you'd
wake to the dazzling glow of,
wild to keep and hold

In front of my mother's vanity

—not the best mirror. If you're not thin at
12 you learn which stores flatter, which
pull thighs wide as corn fields so if some
thing looks ok in them, it's a knock out. The
powder on the vanity is a dusting of snow,
not the deep drifts that will one day bury boxes
of coins, perfume, photographs and letters.
My mother looks up one man's name and
address in any city we're in, and will do so close
to her last day. Her head tilted under the wide-
brimmed black felt hat she knows becomes
her, her lips rose red. After she comes back
with the mail, she'll tuck her skirt up into
underpants I can never believe will be stained,
will terrify. She will half dance around the
apartment as she sweeps and vacuums. She is
singing to Cab Calloway or the music from
Brigadoon and tho my sister and I *"Oh Mother"*
her, embarrassed, she will leap to a table, tap dance
on a stool red paint already is worn from. We don't
imagine years from then people will say, "Your
mother was so much fun," tho I've already read
in her college yearbook all about her phone calls,
her men. My mother's legs are good but we don't
see why she won't keep them covered, tho later I'll
wear miniskirts long after most women don't. Now
I know my mother dances with air because my father,
even when he moved thru rooms as if to take her
by the waist and waltz, won't, as the man I marry
will scowl, "It's the same as to fuck." I take ballet and
pointe to feel I'm moving to music as my mother did,
kicking to balalaikas and strings, not needing a

partner, loving her own legs in five-inch heels or
sneakers, knowing they will take her where she has
to go, that nothing about her is unlovely, just as I will
finally make peace with my legs tho it takes me so long

Lips

"Yours, honey, were so perfect,
a little rosebud mouth, not
those puffed-up blubbery
things," my mother says when
I pointed out the models'
collagen petals. "Roses," my
mother always said, "that's
what yours were, a nice
tiny nose. That's from your
father. One good thing. Not
a big ugly one like I've got."
I think of my mother's lips,
moving close to my hair, how
her breath was always sweet.
"Too thin lips, like your father's,
show stinginess." She was
right. A man who couldn't give
presents or love, a good word
or money. I only remember
three things he told me and
all begin with DON'T tho my
mother said stories came from
those lips, that he brought me a
big dog. I only remember the
thinness of his lips, how his
death meant I wouldn't have to
leave school to testify for the
divorce. Lips. When I came home
from camp I found *Love Without*
Fear in the bathroom and read
"if a girl lets a man put his tongue
on her lips down there, she'll let

him do anything," and then some
thing about deflowering. A
strange word, I thought, trying to
imagine flowers down there, rosebuds
not only on my mouth, a petal
opening, but a whole bush of petals,
a raft of roses someone kneeling
would take me away on, a sea of
roses, flowers and my lips the
island we'd escape to

Tongue

She never told me not to let any
one inside, or that I, like women
in Tibet, who once stuck theirs
out as a greeting for others,
should learn to keep it inside,
sheltered. But the idea of
putting a man inside my
mouth, close to my tongue,

was more than she could
stomach. My mother, who let
me read "Snows of Kilimanjaro"
when my friend's mother would
not, wasn't a prude, but thought
that keeping as much from a man
would just make him want you.
Licking chocolate was one

thing, but to put something you
didn't know where it had been
in your mouth, that was too much.
We had tongue for dinner, that
huge blubbery shape much bigger
than any penis. In her last weeks
my mother craved tongue, not fat,
not too lean but thinly sliced. In our
house, we never held our tongues:
words were razors: *slut*, *liar*,
vicious, *stupid*, were hurled
down the hall like fists or straps.
My mother and I battled, it was
as if we had a body of tongues

stuck out at each other until any
place on our bodies was a mouth

so sore nothing could save us
but to stop each other's mouth
with a long kiss

Eyes

My mother's and mine were
velvety chocolate, like doe's eyes
in candlelight, enormous
over a table. But we couldn't
see, what was ahead was a
blur. What was behind was
haunted. I hated glasses,
pink plastic frames I had
by six, sliding off my nose
and making my too round
face rounder. In photographs
I'm plump, my dark eyes,
even under glasses, like
my mother's while the new
sister's were blue, pale
and her hair blond, her legs
skinny. "Adopted," I often
thought. She was fearless then,
danced in those blue eyes
for strangers while I curled
close to my mother on the
couch, our dark eyes, our soft
bellies. Or I worked quietly,
alone in a room the water-
fall hid, painting, or doing
science projects. Even with a
film over her eyes, she scanned
the length of my skirt, how
I "ruined" my hair, dying and
straightening, saw things
I didn't want her to see. "Your
father's nose," everyone said

but in photographs now I
see my mother looking back
at me, not her presence,
like everyone said I'd feel
being so close, but that dark
glistening polished bark, a
reflection of who I'll be

The jewelry box, the room of lavender and dripping

Otter Creek lulling, spitting damp air
where lilac curtains were taken down. My
mother, older than my grandmother was
when I dreamt and shook in this room,
sits on my old bed, the dusty jewelry
boxes spread open. "You lost so many
of my earrings, honey, but like the
Lindbergh doll you ruined, I let you."
Rhinestones tangle with pins of horses
in the box where a ballet dancer used
to twirl to "Dance, Ballerina, Dance."
My mother pulls a silver dollar to her,
tries to read the date with the one
eye that can. Remember the leaves in the
whirlpool? I held you in this bed when
you moaned with chicken pox, she says;
years after the Nazis I still dreamt they'd
sneak into the house. Rhinestones cloud over
like an eye, the bracelet of Cuban coins from
David before he said "suit yourself" when I
asked if I should wear the yellow evening
gown strapless, then didn't say a thing.
Hearts of rhinestones, silver ballet dancers
for ears, lavender hoops, lavender flowers.
Fraternity pins from loves whose names I
don't remember, rhinestone spray Ron
Agasipour tried to peal from me, like the black
dress of transparent lace in the Middlebury Inn
over where the Junior Women's Club dance
droned on. My mother untwists silver chains
pimply boys thought would make me want
them, says her fingers don't work. "Take them

back now or throw them out," she says of these
fake jewels in their worn cocoons of silk and
velvet as if they were dead babies I could bury
under the floor of my house to wait for their spirit
to bring back what's gone

In Middlebury, the bee man dies

as the geese start to leave,
orchards sagging. The
wind near our old stucco
house two streets away,
steaming with apples.
The bees go on, the
geese remember iced
ponds. When I slept in
the top room with grey
painted boards I heard
horses, could smell
honey in the clover wind
as the bee man walked
thru the hives, bees on
his fingers, the moon's
lemon light on their wings

The bee man's first nights in earth

Now he can see roots
of the clover he carried
home in his arms like a
child, pale branches
trailing toward his lips
and fingers. He hears
the river whose banks
the horses galloped to
under a Harvest moon,
the plink of water like
a xylophone. Wet clay
pools around his fingers
as if to offer a drink. He
misses his bees, his wife's
mango tea with clover
apricot honey, thinks
of flying things that nest
in the ground, hibernate
with the frost. Crystals
already studding his toes
like rings, diamonds
in the black wind

☐ a love of blueness

In front of my mother's vanity

it wasn't my breasts I examined. My mother's big floppy ones,
        strange as
my father's pink bloated penis, seemed less beautiful than smaller
        plum-sized breasts.
Maybe, because I never was anxious, never looked forward to getting
my period, staying small had a similar charm. "Be glad, honey
        you don't have
big boosies like I did," my mother sighed, remembering how,
        in style for the 20s,
she flattened hers with bands. I never cared later that some men
        prefer them

big. It was my legs I hated, didn't trust. They spread out
        on benches for basket-
ball practice to hug each other, as if lonely or afraid to open.
        I longed for thinner legs
like Sally Smith's: her thighs, even pressed together, left an oval
        shape like a pendant
at the ballet barre before she left our high school to be a model
        interviewed on the "Today" show.
Even tanned my legs seemed flabby, blue veins behind my knees
        like road maps to a city
where I had no address, didn't want to go. I picked dresses that

hit mid calf, avoided bathing suits and the beach. By the first round
        of miniskirts,
as my husband kept leaving and each time he did I lost a few pounds,
        tights that could
mold and hold were in and at 103 lbs, suddenly it wasn't my legs
        I tried to hide but my eyes,

red and blotchy. Now, almost as many years from them, like my
        mother's legs,
knockouts èven when she was 70, mine, in latex and nylon,
        preferably black, get me
places I didn't expect to go. When I pass a construction site or walk
        to the metro it's

still "Baby oh-ee" tho I hope they don't get too close to see lines
        where I didn't use to
have them. Yesterday in ballet where I now have that space in my
legs like a 100-lb model, that space I always felt said "I don't need
        to cling, I'm not a whining
baby burying myself in her mother's knees but can move
        on my own, dart,
sprint and leap, balance for as long as I have to," the ballet teacher
said "press your thighs together," I wanted to assure my thighs
        no matter what she says I love them,

not make them feel those words were like a lover who seemed
        to want me, want what I had, wanted me open, wanted
        to enter me, until he had the chance

There should be as many words for loneliness

as Sears makes colors close to rose: Fiesta pink,
dusty rose, camellia, terra cotta, pale rose blush,
pebble, coral light, Tahitian rose, ok coral,
Damask rose, pink carnation. There should be
shades of loneliness like musky rose, maypole
pink—I want more choices, nuances, subtly
different as desert blood from flambeau peach,

Santa Fe peach, shrimp, strawberry, English
cream. The aloneness coming back to the only
dark house on the street where the driveway is
heaped with snow. Or lying alone, in a hospital,
bandaged, my skin ripped. I need skin colors
of rose, the nobody-close-enough-to-reach-out-to
hot ginger, apricot buff, tropic sand. I need
what's as close to but different from peach fuzz,

nasturtium, sunset, musk melon, pomegranate,
a little gladiola and last apricot, apple blossoms
of longing, the softness of rose brown, tongue—
colored laurel. In this stillness give me Turkish
delphinium, rust velvet, the dusky inner lips nobody
feels, so azalea blossom, so Cherokee sunset peach

Though mice have gnawed the green candles

not surprising, the house
still except for the radio
on a timer, the gush of
dripping plants twice a
week. I hope the mice
haven't developed a
taste for sheet music
packed in the garage,
or gone wild for the
letters and poetry mags
nearly toppling over,
shutting out any light.
I'd hate to find they
eat photographs and
posters. I hope that
Maida in my favorite
books is safe, crammed
into herself in the dark,
so unlike her adventures
at camp and in the
theater or going to
Europe or ballet. I
preferred her to Nancy
Drew, found backstage
life more intriguing
than solving who did
what when. I had to take
her from the dusty dry
coves there was rarely
a mouse in, only one
time, a July warm night
when my mother and I

were laughing over some
old boyfriend or thinking
about a pink prom dress
on sale, my first Abyssinian
cat suddenly darted up
toward the cupboard, wild
for the tea cups and then,
one of those huge-eared mice
my mother said she'd never
seen once in the flat (as if
my cat and I brought them)
skittered thru glass. Later
when I found solid evidence,
a skull, small feet in a
dresser drawer and flannel
eaten to lace, it was too late
to tell her. But the mouse
night had its charm: we called
the cops and two came with a huge
steak knife, their patrol-car lights
flashing up Main Street, coaxing
and corralling and finally, with the
suspect wriggling in a paper bag
they left about 2 A.M. and my
mother made black cows and
knew we had a story. When I
packed her house up I couldn't
leave Maida who'd gone places
before me, wasn't a Barbie or a
stewardess or a nurse but wrote
and acted. And is, I hope, safe.
As an artist, she wouldn't mind
the time alone or the quiet.
Two favorite velvet pants were
shredded by squirrels or something

into dust and the fiberglass last
week was shaped for rodent
babies. You were strong, Maida,
even when you didn't get the best
parts and weren't turned into a media
doll to be copied and beheaded.
If you miss the slam of Otter Falls,
be patient. I think you would fit in
down here with the geese on the
pond. Or maybe you could hold
out, work on a new play and we'll
resettle near the ocean where the
tide will rearrange the landscape
you're probably quite bored with

After the house of ghosts

It hurts to come back
and then, like stripping
a bandage off raw skin,
to leave, turn around.
It feels as if I'm facing
away from where I'm
going, pieces of the
house stapled into skin
and nerves. The cat
seems to feel at home,
jumps to the same chair,
eats as she hasn't for
months and may not
again. My mother and
sister move back into my
dreams while the walnuts
die back a few branches
each time, more ragged
and bare against this
March snow that shows
no signs of letting up

Blue Tuesday blues

bluer than blue velveteen,
blue moons, bluer than
a blue letter, bluer than
Canadian Rockies
or clear blue skies.
It's a bitten blue.
Dog Blue blues, Blue boy.
Ladies of the Canyon
Blue. Blue roads,
blue on blue, heartache
blue, a blue raincoat
blue beads fall from,
blueberries, blue eyes
frozen as a blue lake
you skate away on. Blue-
berry Hill blue. Blue
Tuesday. A blue suede
shoes blue, blue baby, blue
blue lace, the old cosmic
blues, blue smoke around
the bed. Old Blue dying
in the backyard blues,
digging his grave. La Fog blue,
blue money. Demon blue.
Blue, blue dress. A
blue Christmas without
you blue, sinking like
poison in Blueberry Lake,
Alaska, an am I blue blues

Tuesday blue

slick as eggplant
of sapphire,
a blue beard melting
over skin without
any color until
the blues takes it.
Royal blue,
bluer than Monday,
darker than antique
typewriter keys
that shatter with
one touch years
after the woman
who first touched
them plunged into
Otter Creek,
the baby a pearl
in her, unraveling
beneath the suede
with matching boots.
Blue ink on
fingers stains
the phone you'd
use ordering out
for Chinese food,
calling 911
after gulping
Valium in a
dream where the
subway out of
darkness lurches
off the track

After not writing much for three months

I need a name like
Estelle or Estralita
for magic, a way to
curl and live in a
lover's hair. Some
one who dissolved
in last night's dream.
Nothing still as a
Vermeer but dazzling,
full of wildness,
a Rousseau. I need a
jump start, words
like *fibulæ* and *retina*,
a Ferrari of a verb.
Somewhere maybe
the sister I no longer
speak with is latching
shutters on a beach
in Maine. I could use
that salt wind, the
grass blown of all
color, hay hair, I
could use language
of the dead to cry on
the shoulder of a
last love. I'd feed him
tropical fruits whose
names are magic,
coco y piña, *mamon*,
empanadas, the sky
a red hemorrhage

Fingers

my mother's on mine in the
car, how, frail, she let her
hand fall down to hold mine
so many years after they
braided with mine dashing
into the ocean, the sky
iridescent, rhinestone water.
Her fingers in my hair
braiding, washing, soothing
my forehead in the weeks
before my sister burst thru
her skin too early, always
insistent on her own time
table. Fingers on my blotched
face and feverish skin, my
mother brought me pineapple
and cherry juice with glass
straws. My mother's fingers,
blue-veined like mine, holding
me as we crossed the street
past rhubarb a babysitter
said wild panthers lurked in.
At Barnstable past reeds and
marsh, roar of the sea, cars
thru littered glass when I
somehow knew she had
more energy than she'd have
again, her fingers, spidery,
wild to hold on, for my
fingers to be the glove
March would be
empty without

A woman goes into the mall

and for whatever reason
disappears beyond velvet
scarves and is not seen
again. Some feel they
hardly knew her, dark
eyes under wheat-colored
hair very much like my
eyes. And she was
wearing my spike heels,
rhinestones. Someone
said they saw her lace,
her shoplifted cashmere.
Another says she was at
the memorial reading,
wrapped in the velvet
she spread over her
long graceful hands. She
had my gloves on, a man
will say. True, my hands
white and thin as hers,
the velvet I'm wearing,
tortoise tissue like roses
always in a clip in my
hair will make you sure
she's me. But listen,
I rarely even finger wool,
not even cashmere, and
the woman at the reading
read my poems in an
accent you might confuse
with mine but I was on
another coast doing

interviews, insisting I
read rarely and only for
a fee, almost tripping in
those four-inch glittery heels.

Metro, January 8

across the rails, the man
with long black hair and
flashing eyes and a smile
I'd have found as devastating
as the blond on his neck,
voice full of flamenco and
Lorca, castanets. She is
as pale as he is darkly onyx,
skin a creamy caramel. "I've
seen you, yes often," I hear
her say as she inches closer
and then shakes hands. He
moves as if every space he
knows will warm and open
to him. She's smiling. Laughs
a little too much, her green
parka seems to be reaching
to touch him as if, if she does
not move fast, he'll dissolve,
and I think of myself, leaving
a radio station and not wanting
to go without a hook in the
man who made me as breathless
as I feel her becoming. "We
could have coffee," I say,
meaning *my number*, mean-
ing *just ask*. The curve of
my body so like hers as the
train doors open, heading for
a seat where two could fit. Her
voice full of stories, holding
him as I knew my pink lips

over rose leather saying who-
knows-what did to the man
on the air, made of air like
those streamers immigrants
leaving Europe on a boat
tied to someone on shore,
floating on currents
of air like skywriting,
a plea even after the ship's
out of sight and those
on shore stare into blackness

Another woman who looks like me

gets on Amtrak, leaves
her suitcase on the
platform. Nobody she
leaves behind has a clue.
She isn't a terrorist,
there's no Anthrax or
fertilizer in it, only
a few explosive
words to someone
dead. She could have
just made a fire,
curled near the etched
glass as if nothing
had happened
yet or revised the past.
But instead, she's coiled
what no one is left
to understand in the
lingerie pockets of a
shattered blue suitcase.
You might think
she's reckless
or lost, in a daze, but
first imagine she
sees it as a child too
much for her that
she can't bear to keep
or know will grow
up with strangers
so before it can
belong to anybody
else, she wraps the

words in lamb's wool
like someone
putting a newborn
in thick wool,
leaving it in a
dumpster with a
diamond anklet to
let whoever takes it
know how much
it mattered

I wear my hair long

to remember old boyfriends'
aunts making appointments,
telling stylists to cut it short,
in a flip. I wear my hair long
to protest against all the
shaved heads at Auschwitz,
against the threats of PhD
examiners to look more
professional and dignified.
I want it to smell of lilac wind,
want my old cat in its warmth.
I long to hang my hair out
windows to shy lovers, a
dare, a disguise to throw you
off. I envy Indian women
who can sit on the black river
pouring down their backs.
My hair begs to be touched,
caught in your fingers,
your teeth. It smells of lilies,
gardenias, some animal you
never want not near once
you've stroked it. Taste
it and you'll want to wear
it, wrap dreams deep in it
when leaves start to change.
Pale as a flag made of the
moon it will guide you, lead
you in deeper

☐ written on the body of night

Venice Daphne run backwards

the way that sandpiper runs
as close to the water
and then knows, pulls
back, but not
before he's dug
into sea grass. I'm
walking out of branches,
wood, Daphne
run backwards, my own
breakwater this time.
Blue shells, sun
cupped in the arm of some-
one who doesn't own
or want to own me.
The leaves he pulls from
my skin are stained
with the verbs of someone
who didn't see what she could.
Salt air chews them.
We dream of Nantucket,
wine in a grey wood
someday. You know I never
wanted a man just
for myself
but didn't know that.
Gulls. Old women
unbutton black coats,
feel the light, dreams moving
in their throat like birds.
They are willow roots

hanging on under
the sand, pushing deep.
In this light, if they
were to unloosen a few
pins they would grow into
their hair, birds blown in the
sun toward cities rarely
found on maps

E-mail message

"I love the idea of you
putting quilts on your
plants, a yard of quilts
like a front-yard bed
and you tucking in your
plants for naps." The
just turned earth, your
just turned earth. You
won't need a quilt,
you never liked any
thing too near the foot
that was mangled. The
other, buried in Nam.
I tucked the basil in,
covered cilantro and
chives, the wind a
lullaby getting some-
thing ready for sleep or
dying, really the same
holding and wrapping
as the dark grows

Black sweater in May

pulling the sun in close.
That other May
the rose apple was
almost startling;

I'd slept alone in
the west side of the
house, sloped
ceiling across the bed,
not wanting to hear
glass when a bottle
slammed thru it.

The sun warmer
than hands, it slid
thru the last
mounds of snow as the
man who made me blush
just sitting near me

was suddenly there. I
hadn't seen him walking
toward where he'd
touch my shoulder,
tell me the name for
the tree I thought
was dogwood, pull

me toward his small
warm room that
night when it was
black and the grass
was black, wet, a
sweet smell I don't
remember smelling
since

The apple orchard man

I saw him four times
in my grandfather's dept
store's triple mirror,
my own cheeks pinker
than my pink piqué
dress. Fluorescent
lights, mountains of
house dresses still
hugging the week's heat,
he strutted down aisles
of Levis. No matter,
later I heard he
was on drugs, had
three wives. When he
leaned a hip toward
me, his grin of other
dark charming men I'd
never see as danger,
I could have invited him
into the stuffy dressing
room as if that close
dark was a part of me
and I'd been waiting.
I longed to lie under
his branches, have the
dark fruit glisten over
my body, saw myself
brushing long mahogany
hair in a window over
the orchard, everything in
me wild petals he could
open and coax to
bloom as wildly

The first time

not in a marriage bed but
in a motel I could walk to
from that raised ranch my
husband and I played house
in. Virgins for years after
the wedding until I taunted
a man with words, the only
way I knew, got him to
slither in broken shoes from
another coast. I didn't know
if he really was an ex-con.
He looked like a stud. He
couldn't believe he had me
first, rocked back on his
knees in the motel as cars
honked by. I didn't know if
he could kill me, what I'd
get from him. Or that I
would not feel different,
would not feel much. I
looked in the mirror, felt
his tongue along my mouth.
Already I was longing for
quiet afternoons alone
while this large man who
wouldn't fit anywhere
slogged a beer, grinned,
said he kept tasting me

From the mattress on the floor under the flaming sky photo

rain blurs moon
and stars, eyes dark
as licorice like water
in an old mine. A
stranger reading
Lorca in Spanish on
the phone. Later my
hands smelled like
him, cinnamon
skin. The dog barked
thru damp sheets.
I got wet, fingers
on my skin. *"You all
horned up,"* whispering.
If I'd thought
twice I wouldn't
have, in my leather
skirt and high
heels, pink *"what
are those,
barrettes?"* he
asked pulling rose
clips from my hair.
"And your scent," he was
pressing the strangest
flowers, pulled
my hair, tilted
forsythia dripping like
my hair, I fell out
of what held me

Dream of smoke and orchids
or, After 24 hours with the stranger who is still
in Nam in his head

my phone rings all
night. Friday is
an envelope that
went thru the
wash with the
only number I
needed on it.
When I try to
talk, just
static. My
stories wilt
like an orchid
yanked out of
green ferns,
left in a locked-
up vinyl front seat
sun bakes 17
hours. I didn't
give my last
name but sent
clues daily,
left rose and jasmine
scent for a
trail of crumbs,
but the last digit
was phony. Now
the phone rings:
a fire alarm, the
wires smoking.
I put on gloves,

unlist my lips.
I refuse to care,
aching to do
anything flip.
But don't
hang up

The man who brought emerald mandarin oranges

because they
were the color
of his eyes
and he could feel my
legs turn
to sea water.
He was leaning too
close, knew I wanted
to. His eyes whole
oceans full of
crinkly fish.
He wore light green
clothes. Wheat
was what he cared
for, buying and
selling. He knew the
green would be
striking against a
field of wheat,
startling as when he
moved near me
on the couch. Green
eyes of water. Sea
that dazzles, pulls cars
off Route 1A, his
hair black, blacker
than rocks
at Big Sur

Rescued again

Above Paradise,
late, slamming
in again. Not at
all what I'd
expected. My
leather hip clutched
past pool tables,
brass and strings.
I could have been
on the late-night-
into-early-morning
bus, stumbling,
dazed that time not
by dark but by
light, the Pacific.
Ice plant glowing,
you there when
someone wasn't.
Suddenly I was in your
room of just one
bed and now enough
years later I could
have had a daughter
small enough for
that 18-year-old skirt
but don't, so
I wear it, stumble
from the bathroom
as if from that
bus and you're
reaching out, there,
in the black of

noise and night
and pin balls
Above Paradise
smiling,
holding me

The man who says floating blonds come thru his eyes

doesn't really want one
for more than a night.
They're like pillows or
quilts. After all, he says,
you can only fuck
so much. He prefers men,
hard thighs, calloused
fingers, a six-pack with
two guys, the works
on the deck where light
goes amber and blush,
prefers his hair tossed
by salt wind. Women
for him are sad and
grieving. Men know its
one nail, one board
after another, a little
mortar, cement. Even
cats know what women
never will. He's soothed
by sage and anise in the
canyon, the stillness
alone after work, sheets
clean as new plaster

It was better, he said

than Christmas with
that half-naked girl,
her tongue down
his throat while
the record stuck on
Elvis's "Blue Christmas."
When he forgot the
language, he couldn't
remember how it
seemed, only how her
leg caught his lips
on the stained sofa
that you could smell
ancient sex smells rise
from like fish-egg
smell over Orleans
where the sea's blue
in the mirror was
less blue than her veins

"The wholesale artificial limbs business," she says, "that sounds like a poem, a book," and I think how it was

the one story I could tell
the famous novelist in the
colony where the bush
that looked like roses but
wasn't was the color
of the sweater I wore
sitting under it, color
of the inside of a mouth
when he walked by and
told me the name of
the tree I used to think
was forsythia, asked
about a drink after 9.
His study past the black
dripping berry branches,
the glass of scotch, a
candle I clasped as if it
was close to freezing and
there was no place to go
but his sheets. I was too
in awe to talk, his name
a throbbing organ I'd
never resist but like a
tray of flowers or platter
of shrimp I'd decorated
with actual rubies, I
could have curtseyed to
his applause of my story
of our shared relative
who, yes, sold artificial
hips and limbs

Expulsion from the garden

I thought it was
odd at first. *Take
off your clothes* you
said, unbuttoning yours,
putting the Polaroid
on a timer.

We laughed about what
would turn up. One

caught us
moving. But the other,

my hand touching you
lightly, chilled.

We didn't expect any
thing so haunting,

strangely like Masaccio's
Adam and Eve

Two Thursdays

We should have thought,
I could have been
sketching you all
this time

you tell me my
breasts are glistening,
take off the lilac
shirt and I lay there
hardly noticing mosquitoes,
the wool

If I say lie could I
lose this blue, could
I feel more like I
did then

thinking damp thoughts

the Chianti in an
old clay jar,
your cool shoulders

Lemon sun, Saturday

wind chimes

Jenny's slightly sour
sheets

the few white hairs on
your chest
      I'm sorry I couldn't
forget
and swing, but my eyes
      were burning

lying now, this mattress
in your old friends' house

lemon sun, Billy's
TENNESSEE BLUES
thru the shade. He's been

playing since midnight

Jenny standing in the
door, parting the
curtains slowly

Rich dark

No slivering streetlight
through heavy curtains,
but the feel of your thigh
smooth through the sheet.
In the light your hair's
hot amber, now wild
seaweed, silky smelling,
like lemons and the pillow
smells of your skin. Only
willow sounds on the
screen till suddenly you
move away, stumbling to
where the light goes on
and the rich dark stops

That February

snow on our hair,
the room so warm and
everything melting,
there thoughts of
starting but it was all
over, that's the way it
had to stay. Dust
in our throats, the same
dried flowers on the wall
and we leaving, half relieved,
clutching iced branches
glad for the cold

Blue Sunday

imagining that he slips
from her the way rings
do from a finger in
the cold. Leaves. October,
black spots on the mirror.
Separation blues in the
bed. Touching his shoulders
here on paper, he's like
all the flowers that I
draw, bright wild petals
that don't connect to
any stem

Those nights

branches across the
clouds could have
been antlers. Of
course they were
just trees. Arms

were arms. You
were dark as your
hair, blue as your
sea eyes. It was
not always like

talking to some
one in a coffin.
Your stories
wrapped me in
green like grape

leaves. Afterwards,
it was often like
having a beautiful
dress, pale lace
tangling at my feet

so I couldn't move

Dialing your number

something froze
as if I'd walked
unprepared
into a calculus test in
some nightmare, or
as if I were that man

singing "Ave Maria"
in the death camp
near a quarry who,
just as he hits the high
note, feels the ledge
beneath his worn shoes

crumble away. I'm
astonished that the
number is not dead,
is not disconnected,
since everything else
is: I've left town, and

you've left the airwaves.
When it rings and rings
and rings, I'm flung
back to a time when
your fingers picked up
the receiver—your fingers

part of me then, it seemed—
but now as distant as
the thought of buffalo
on the moon, buffalo

you know aren't there
but that you see

quite clearly nonetheless
thru the gauze of 2 A.M.
and the wind-blown lace
curtain, their sad eyes
stunned by the knowledge
that they are only phantoms

This time I can leave you

but what? Not stones
like in a Jewish cemetery.
I forget if there are
flowers in Arlington.
LEAVE ME ALONE
is what you said you
wanted. Now, beyond
weather or flowers,
you have plenty of time
to wait as I did often,
mornings you'd decide
you weren't in the
mood. It won't
bother you,
nothing will

A woman went into the cemetery

disappeared behind granite
and was never heard from
again. We don't quite
believe this. She could
have gone to the museum
or called her girlfriend
to meet her for lunch
but instead took the
metro to the cemetery
as if to lie down with the
dead one who always said
her lips brought him
back to life. It was a warm
day for December even
tho it was the day of
the least light. She was
wearing the denim mini
I had in my closet,
her hair almost as long
and red as mine. Some might
suppose I was that woman,
it seems there were clues.
But listen, the buried
man was already dead to
me before he slept
under the grave in this
city and the me who would
have banged myself
raw on his metal
door had already grown
skin too thick to feel

Everything I have you don't have

—hunger, sleepiness, anxiety,
regret, bad dreams, terror.
Even when you were living
it was like talking to a corpse.
You don't need to shower
or eat. It's not that you needed
much before, a room with a
cot and cardboard nightstand.
Radio people have to be
able to quickly move, go.
Having a lot is an albatross
especially when it comes to
women who might want to see
you more than twice. You
won't need your Zanex under-
ground, can't tease about
Valium in the shape of a heart.
You won't have to walk point.
You won't have to walk, won't
need that fake leg. I think of you
watching the roots move closer,
circle your bones like a women's
legs, now in a room darker than
you kept yours so you could
sleep at noon after all night on
the air. You won't see this
long spring, the roses unfolding,
clenched tiny buds opening
petal by petal as I longed to

I never wanted you

to stay with me
longer. I was anxious
to be alone, go over
the frames like some-
one picking up photo-
graphs of a place they
are not sure they will
go back to. Sleeping
with you was the
best part, actually
being asleep, coiled
with your arms
around me as if even
afterward you wanted
to pull me near. Now
I'm too often nervous,
leave bits of my skin,
crumbs of myself,
so you can trail me.
I wonder, from this
distance, how I look
to you? Like a ghost,
that exotic light on a
moon you could navigate
by? Or, face to face,
would you still back
away as if you needed
distance to notice
my intensity?

Now you've spent a whole month in the ground

past muscle memory.
In ballet the tendons
and sinews store move-
ment, a hard drive whose
files cannot be erased.
Phantom pain, an
old story. But what
of the tissues
connected to what
is now gone, a leg
that exploded across
a minefield, there
and not there, like
a lover who says it's
not you and dissolves?
With you, I was like
a Siamese twin who
survives the other
but never heals, burns,
stays raw where the
hearts and lungs
once connected

I read in a clip that your son said you'd have liked

the peaceful snow that
fell the day you died,
the day you were
buried. I fly back to
the snow you drove
to pick me up in,
how it blanketed
Sunday as you did
tho chunks of
terror, ice shoves
that would bury
both our houses,
were still under
the skin of white

White trees in the distance

a white wind of
petals, maybe snow.
The longest I've
been so close to
you on the sheet
of paper. Like your
death, these poems
about you, a wild
surprise. The last
page in the note-
book; still I think
I'll need another
notebook before I
can let you go

"Kiss, Baby," the new film

an obsession much more rare than mine, tho
in some ways not that different. The woman
in love with what's dead, what's given up
on breathing, caring, could be me knocking
my knuckles raw on your metal door while
you gulp another beer, put your head down
on the table. With you, it often was like
singing to someone in a casket the lid was
already down on, still expecting something.
She buried animals in the woods, didn't mind
touching them. Though I made our nights into
something more, I could have been coiled
close to a corpse. No, that part is a lie. Your
body was still warm. It was everything inside
where your heart must have been that was
rigid, icy. The woman in the film went to work,
an embalming assistant. Isn't that what I'm
doing? Preserving you with words? Making
love to you on these sheets of paper, a tentative
kiss on cold lips, cuddling a cadaver?
In the film, the woman says loving the dead is
"like looking into the sun without going blind,
is like diving into a lake, sudden cold, then
silence." She says it is addictive. I know about
the cold and quiet afterward, how you were a
drug. If she was spellbound by the dead, who
would say I wasn't, trying to revive, resuscitate
someone not alive, who couldn't feel or care,
the uninhabited shell of a body. Here, where no-
body can see, I could be licking your dead body
while driving thru a car wash, I could be whispering
to the man across the aisle, "Bodies are addictive."

Our word for the loved is the same as for the dead,
the beloved, and once you've had either while you
have them, you don't need any other living people
in your life

Like the woman wild to have calligraphy

done all over her body,
these notebooks could
be your skin. Now that
you're dead, I can make
up what you want, and
when you want it. Each
verb's a finger, a tongue,
the pen, a greeting, a kiss
hello or goodby. See how
I've used so many colors,
brushed the face I remember
with blues and onyx. I
imagine you under the
roses dreaming of
calligraphy, of the way I
move over you as if you
are what I write

When I read about another woman whose pleasure came

from texts written on
her body, who takes a series
of calligraphers as lovers
because her father used
to write traditional
greetings on her face,
I thought of how it was
your words coming thru
the radio that might have
been fingers, not on skin
or thighs but on my mind,
pulling me close to your lips,
a magnet midnight to dawn
before I ever saw your ice-
blue-lake eyes no one could
skate over without danger
of drowning, you stroked
and soothed, sucked
on every part of me
opening for more

Moving by touch

almost, as tho it
was the leaves, grey
all afternoon. Could
it have been the water
moving near us
pulled us together
so that that night
warm in each other's
hair, roots were
sprouting from a
moist dark? It was
so strange, even later
we didn't know
what to call that
need or love
like mushrooms,
overnight,
not expected

*

quietly
pressing frost
off to touch
the taste,
feel of
iced glass. The
apples in the
sun window
where the
paint is
peeling

shine
the way we
lean here
saying
nothing
but know

*

living with
you, well this
room's not
everywhere, I
know there are
other places.
Right now I don't want to go

*

let me I
know the chilly
places in you, I
never wanted to
marry you
away from those
wild caves

here there's
dogwood now,
I'm thinking how
I was the one
scared then

you carried me,
I know the snow
would sting
if you
let go

None of
that matters

The origin of the seasons according to the Delawares

A man and a woman
lived together,
started fighting.
It was far north
and cold so she went
into the hotlands.
But he got lonely,
rode south to take
her back. He brought
the cold with him;
wherever he went
it was winter. They
did this every year

When they wheeled you away

and the elevator door
slammed shut, it was
like a mother handing
a child over in wartime
to strangers he might
be safe with. Suddenly
masked figures in
green owned you,
would have their
way with you like
someone hacking up
bodies. Those wartime
women, too, must have
been uncertain they would
see what they loved
again. I would have
been the one that
never had wanted
children, was bullied
and conned. Then
couldn't imagine her
child in another's
arms, gone

When he says you never write any good poems about me

I think by "good" he means "sexy." Poems
about stopping on back roads in the car with
a bigger front seat, not even waiting for
a road off a road but pulling velvet and denim
off like roast skin from a turkey. I don't tell
him, maybe I should, but the poems dripping
love juice and pubic hair were written when
I wasn't getting any. A virgin after eight years,

my mind was never not on erotic movies in
my head where even the music was the in and
out of bodies. I had time in the raised ranch
to dream a man would emerge from the trees,
fantasize slow afternoons behind chiffon drapes
in the bed of white silk until it ripped. Years my
arms ached for more than the tiger cats and
the buff kitten. If a man wrote me from some

coast I opened on paper to him, came on to
strangers and convicts on the page. Those sheets
always felt safe enough to let them know their
words got me wet, even my hair was horny. I
wrote about what wasn't there, what left a hole
I was terrified I'd drown in. "Writing like a hippie
but living like a nun," a magazine quoted me and
probably I said it. It was the way those in

the concentration camp talked of food, of seeing
light, the moon, were famished for the smell of
bread. Fantasized chicken, apples, beef, all the things
they'd never thought much about when they had
more than they could devour as, baby, I do now

When I think of him leaving

I imagine I'll go first, roll
the Persian rugs into a
wheelbarrow I can bury
the computer in, take out
to the woods past the pond.
Poems will be full of the
moon, a little pine, hickory.
Nobody to tell me to turn
off the radio, the light.
Some nights I take inventory,
move deeper into the teal
and mauve of the rug,
the wild reds spattered thru
slate like a map with symbols
in code, something from the
16th century where a woman
was beaten by her husband or,
worse, had her tongue cut
out. Though no longer able to
tell the story with her mouth,
she wove the blood tale between
peacocks and willows. If I feel
alone in the trees I will
wrap in their warmth,
bring their mystery into poems
that will take on the scent of
night magnolias and dark mahogany

☐ parallel worlds

I think of my grandfather

on a cramped ship
headed toward Ellis Island.
Fog, foghorns for a
lullaby. The black
pines, a frozen pear.
Straw roofs on fire.
If there were postcards
from the sea there might
have been a *Dear
Hannah* or *Mama*, hand
colored with salt.
*I will come and get you.
If the branches are
green, pick the apples.
When I write next, I will
have a pack on my
back, string and tin.
I dream about the snow
in the mountains. I never
liked it but I dream of
you tying a scarf
around my hair, your
words that white dust*

If my grandmother could have written
a postcard to Odessa

She would write her
name in salt, salt
and mist, an SOS
from the ship sea
wind slaps with night
water. *Somehow I'm*
dreaming of Russian
pines. I don't dream
of the houses on fire,
babies pressed into
a shivering woman's
chest to keep them
still. Someone had
something to eat the
color of sun going
down behind the
hill late summer,
orange, with its own
sweet skin. They
are everywhere in
America. If the roses
ever bloom in our
town of darkness,
just one petal in an
envelope would be
enough

From the first weeks in New York, if my grandfather could have written a postcard

if he had the words, the
language. If he could
spell. If he wasn't only
selling pencils but knew
how to use them, make
the shapes for words
he doesn't know. If he
was not weighed down
with a pack that made
red marks on his shoulder,
rubbed the skin that
grew pale under layers
of wet wool, he might have
taken the brown wrapping
paper and tried to write
three lines in Russian
to a mother or aunt he
might never see again.
But instead, too tired to
wash hair smelling of
burning leaves he walked
thru, he curled up in a
blue quilt, all that remained
of the cottage he fled
that night running past
straw roofs on fire, and
dreamt of those tall black
pines but not of how, not
yet 17, he will one day live
in a house that he will own,
more grand than any he
saw in the old country

May 10

my grandmother's birthday
and the day they gave my
father for his birthday,
all records lost leaving
Vilnius. I think of my
grandmother in a house
the maples already
towered above hearing
the news the first day it
might have been warm
enough to sit out on the
glider, feeling a chill,
wrapping the rainbow
afghan around her, her
youngest just in his teens,
almost close enough
to have to leave her. She
will stop sleeping, answer
the phone with a terrified
what's wrong as blood
and snow spirea open
and the peonies that will
outlast her and her boy
fill with ants that you can
see from the glider only
as a faint shadow

The other fathers

would be coming back
from some war, sending
back stuffed birds or
a handkerchief in navy
blue with *Love* painted
on it. Some sent telegrams
for birthdays, the pasted
letters like jewels. The
magazines for children
were full of fathers who
were doing what had
to be done, were serving,
were brave. Someone
said there'd be confetti
in the streets and maybe
no school, that soon we'd
have bananas. My father
sat in the grey chair,
war after war, hardly
said a word at dinner. I
wished he had gone away
with the others so maybe
he would be coming
back to us

Like some lies we tell ourselves

the story of my father
on the phone, invited to
my wedding, bloomed then
settled into the landscape.
He's your father, boy-
friends would say, *don't
you feel something? He
showed your poems to
Frost.* The image of my
father in a chair listening
to the Dow Jones, saying
nothing, hangs in the air
but yesterday I found
that letter I wrote
after my husband-to-be
called and my father
blurted: *I don't care
about her. I don't want
to come to your wedding,
hear about it, be involved.
And I don't want to pay.*
It flares open, a yucca
plant that takes 100 years
to bloom, floods the night
with a peculiar scent and
I think how I've hated
cheap men, one sign and
I'm running. I think how,
dead so long, even today
my father takes up too
much space

Wooden medicine cabinet

behind the toilet, not the
one for toothpaste and soap,
but higher, with a lock
where my mother would
have kept a diaphragm if
she had one, my father's
old shaving brush, 33 years
after its sable touched his
skin, crammed in the back
like an aunt who isn't quite
right in some upstairs bedroom.
There, behind talcum powder
no longer made, Vaseline
that's gone ochre. If there
were condoms, my mother
would have thrown them out,
as if at 52 she wouldn't have
anyone else, but maybe she
thought that soft brush, bent
back by my father's skin as
she had been, could stay,
a ghost of the little he
had let close

My father's wallet

Maybe he abandoned it long before he abandoned us.
He lived in the same house, moving past us in the hall,
sat without a word at the chrome kitchen table until
my mother moved out first, took a spring cottage at the
lake where my cat got treed and firemen came to rescue.
After that, Othello was not let off the porch. By summer,
we were back in our own apartment and my father took
rooms at a house in town, hitched up and down Rte 7 after
my mother took his key to the Pontiac. To break the
gloom, I thought I would marry and invited him to come.
"I don't want to be involved or to pay," he hissed on the
phone, the last words he'd say to me except, once when
I ran into him in the post office and he whispered,
"Don't do anything you don't want." He hadn't even
wanted to send my sister or me to college, just cared
about the stocks, wanted them to be a memorial to him,
never go to his wife or daughters but simply go on maturing
until the world collapsed like a spaceship lost in orbit,
circling endlessly with no way to escape. This wallet
must have been as much a time capsule of what he
could walk away from as easily as his heart did from us,
with its birth certificate listing a date I never knew and
the town of Viloa in the county of Vilna, a page that
looked like an old Confederate bill, a few pennies from
the 20s, as useless to him as I guess we were

The cousins' party

One Sunday every August my mother's cousins
came with photographs from summers they
camped out on North Pleasant, my grand-
mother making lemon meringue pie, which my mother
ordered in restaurants and always found wanting.
The last time I drove up, a lover's scent
still in my hair, my lace still smelling of him,

leaves tipped with red. Suddenly, the cousins
began to go and my mother couldn't swallow.
Then one cousin went into the hospital for some-
thing minor and didn't return. Kay, who loved my
poems, had fought so many parts of her being
poked at and sliced away but always made up
and with a new wig, smiling and dancing,

suddenly couldn't go on anymore. They skipped
the party for a year when another cousin fell
and couldn't remember his own name and Kay's husband
(always her lover, the one she talked about putting on
sexy lingerie for even while having chemo, the one she
wore a wig for even when she slept) fell over in a day
and uncles started coughing, gasping for air they'll never
        get again.

Like birds migrating—as if they got a signal, some
radar, or saw something in the leaves—they're on
their way, like they were in other summers, packing the
old Ford for Atlantic City, Chicago World's Fair 1939,
in Panama hats and navy middy dresses, everyone
going, not wanting to be left behind

Vacation

Often, my sister in the car,
her arms folded across
her heart to be sure
no one could get there.
At restaurants she ate only
tuna and bologna. I curled
as far away as I could
from the snakes of
smoke in the back seat,
wanted to be suspended
between where we
came from and where we
were headed, which could
never live up to what
we dreamed. Sometimes our
parents didn't squabble.
Sometimes my father
forgot to write down the
cost of each meal and
my mother didn't have to
coax and beg him to
go to the Music Tent. Some-
times he looked as if he
was actually enjoying
Brigadoon or *Oklahoma!*
and my sister came into the
restaurant to try pizza,
didn't just pout in the car,
and tho a few years later
I sulked a little when
they wouldn't let me go out
on a date with boys I met

on the miniature golf course,
each time we left for home
we ached and longed for
the salt air, the beach plum
and roses, waves on the
black rocks blurring
what we didn't want
to hear

My sister's birthday

In photographs
of us in pinafores
on the piano,
enough years
for us to have
had our own
daughters in
caramel and
butterscotch
stripes, my
sister and I
coil into my
mother's black
dress, into
her smile, her
white teeth a
beacon. We
looked to her
to know the way
until my sister
didn't. My
mother named
her Hope in
the middle of
what must have
been her own
sadness. Hope,
there too early,
demanding air,
rattling every-
body, wild to

have her own
way and making
chaos as she
would

She was two when she locked the bathroom door behind her

tearing my mother up,
making my father climb
to the roof next door,
go thru the motions of
flipping the bolt to the left.
He begged and pleaded,
cajoled, coddled, waited.
Somehow they opened
that door but they couldn't
open others deep inside her,
past the blonde-beauty
hair, the blue eyes that made
me sure she was adopted.
She locked doors in her
head, ran with horses,
men who would or
would not leave their wives,
lashed out, bruising,
bruised, suing leaves off
the tree, suing the sun
for daring to enter. She
blocked windows, caged
cats, caged herself
behind pounds that hid
her once perfect body.
She put up bars, double-
locked her nightmares,
flung her fists like an
infant cutting the air into

shreds, fists as fast as the
blades of a fan you can't
tell are spinning in circles
unless you get too near

My sister's film

It's a crackly home movie
my sister has held hostage for
nearly 30 years and will
allow our mother only a
glimpse of when she knows
there won't be another
chance. Like a 50-year-
old who gives a flash of
what she's hid so long
it's no longer what lips
and fingers and eyes
are wild for, she
decides to put it all in
hiding again, stashes
mother's black curls back,
my wedding gown being
buttoned, rewinds my long
mahogany hair that hangs
thickly past pink velvet,
yanks back mother's escape
from geese, locks all she
has left of when we still
held each other, held
on, holds them like some-
one kidnapped, like loot
from a hold up, as dogwood
berries turn red in the
fall, dark blood berries
the birds lust for

Images of my cousin

haunt the way
in certain light
or when wind comes
up behind
something dead
on the highway
moves still,
seems alive.
In dreams my
cousin is
thin again,
giggling, hasn't
called the police,
spit "selfish
bitch." July is
lilacs still
in the cold hills.
August hasn't
exploded like
pieces of a
scattered bird

September 23, 1996

A red tide in Texas, a
red tide between my
sister and me. This day
of forgiveness, we
don't talk, haven't.
I wonder if she's
beginning another
diet with a fast. Or
maybe she's gotten
rid of her fat the way
she shed most of her
family. I wonder if she
has dyed her hair, is
rigging up telescopes,
saving refugees or
walling herself in with
acres of Holocaust
books, cages to lock
her turtles in. Towels
over the window. No
one is sure where the
poison in the tide
comes from, what to
do with it, how long
it will ruin things

Hearing my cousin

whom I haven't talked
to for over a year
looked scrawny again,
her hair straggly at
the church four days
after finding her father-
in-law still warm but
dead under blue sheets
just after breakfast.
I think of my cousin
at the last party, her
hair sleek, her white
teeth looking like she
could be her husband's
child. The father-in-law,
there eating toast and
then slipping from them
as my cousin has from
me. She was wearing a
frumpy long dress, my
mother tells me. She
was crying, the dead
branches out in the
maple still holding
their leaves. My mother
says her husband held
her so tight. The phone
sweaty in my hands from
holding it harder than
I knew I held it

If you read her life backwards in dripping lilacs

pressed against glass,
snow hairs turning
blonder. Fat pulls
from bones that
used to split in the
air on ice, they
lose their stiffness,
unbend like her
lips pursed in a
frown. Terror of
leaving the house
or flying sands
itself away.
She is flying over
the Caspian in her
own Cessna 12, whoosh-
ing upward, dreams
of the man who
will see her thighs
as something more than
what a paper sheet
covers before they're
opened, explored
with metal and light,
before his touch
becomes real,
frightening

Photographs in my mother's pocketbook

Just my sister and
me, but not together,
as now. After our mother's
death, it's not likely
we will be. The edges
are frayed, Polaroids
losing their color. One,
me in my wedding gown,
is folded across the
forehead as if predicting
the scar where the
car's glass and metal
will gnaw. My sister is
blonde, mostly skinny
tho one with a braid
looks ahead to when
she's chunky. I'm 16,
I'm 23, I'm 30, look
more interesting as I
plunge ahead. French
twists, braids, beehives.
Curl Free—straight hair
with rhinestones, pearls,
lace. Shifts, gowns,
stripes, cashmere and
velvet. My sister and I
clutching flowers,
pocketbooks, perfect
skin as if we knew
none of it could last

The blue candy dish

Soon it will be
eight years, it's like
nothing. The hours wrapping
glasses from the 50s,
each sail of red flung
me back like a wrinkle
no surgery repairs.
Each lilac blossom slammed
her back to the New York
City place, the man who wrote
his pain on pale blue folded
paper. If lilacs came in blue
she would have had them. The
blue violin candy dish in pieces.
If my sister and I still talked,
I could ask her if she
remembers how or when.
Now even finding
the cover blurs like
outlines in a silver pond, doves
in the leaves. In photographs
maybe, still, what I was
willing to lose. Vultures at the garage
sale, before the magnolias, how I
rescued the pigeon ruby punch bowl
but let the blue candy-dish cover go,
dazed from hours of packing and
unpacking. Someone up three
nights, on a train more like
a cattle car, lulled
by night birds, dreaming
of a night that happened

long enough ago to have been
in another life but more
real than the trains'
wail in blackness

My uncle sells the store

long dark aisles where
I used to pick new
sweaters and specially
ordered wool skirts
too itchy to wear
from hangers and lug
upstairs as if
picking wild flowers
in Bataille Woods. White
piqué I thought it was
dumb for me to have with
my plump arms and
belly, cotton that would
have looked so much better
on someone thin like Vivian
or Gina before the car
sliced her body and
no one could quite get it
back. Hot musty corners
where my father lurked
quietly in back of tall
mountains of shoeboxes
writing stock tips like
secret letters to a mistress.
My mother had played in
these shadows where
salesmen trying to sell
corsets and black bras
whispered "merry widow"
when my mother began to
get breasts and put their eyes
and hands where they should

not, her face burning like
the mahogany shelves that
March when the wood and
cash registers exploded as if
there was too much unsaid
and darkly secret in
the hills and caves of
Capezio shoes and yarn
to go on

Not half as much but double

my father collapses 12 days before
court and the divorce, his nose
a broken flower in snow on the
hills near the Episcopal church.
Years later my mother says she
called him 2 nights before in the
room he rented from someone in
town but when she heard his voice
she hung up so the stocks weren't
divided tho he owed a lot. She
said it took years to pay off, wrote
one will dividing what she had
in two, a half for each daughter
until my sister sued me for a poem,
might as well have pulled a knife
on my mother's dreams in the
years they didn't talk. My mother
redid the will, another half twisted
to a whole, or nearly, a relief as
etched with loss (and what isn't?)
as the etched glass I'm packing, dark
as tarnished silver, split, crazed as
old glass that was once one piece,
won't be

My uncle is dead

Scientists say everything is getting farther from
everything else, darker, more lonely. The center
of gravity is loosening, letting go. I feel my
mother drifting further into darkness. My uncle
tries to catch up. I don't talk to my sister. Repulsive

and unexpected forces, a Pandora's box, the paper
says. Imagine being a raisin in a loaf where
the dough is baking, rising, the other raisins,
unloosened, now farther away. Today you forgot
to put out vitamins for me, a small act I take as

love, as my mother measured each extra
degree of heat as caring. Then, you forgot the
mail, told me I didn't load the dishwasher
right, talked when you were in a room where you
couldn't hear. I wanted to leave a message on

your voice mail but a ghost voice said, "All
space is gone." Scientists say now space will be
emptier, lonelier. After the operation, we had
no galaxies except the bottom room where you
rested in a chair under the lion blanket, grateful

for soup and tea. Each complication sucked us
closer: the gravity of irregular heartbeats,
temperature over normal narrowed our universe to
a cove of down quilts, pillows that shut out the
world. When you first walked to work it seemed

a miracle, but now with gravity dissolving, I feel
like an abandoned raisin, no other raisin close
enough to touch

The past is melting in my fingers

My mother is talking to the cat in the
hallway before heat moves in. She is
70, she says she could never swallow,
can't imagine caring if you don't
make a man's thing feel like a tongue
on fire. She is 50, a widow, her perfect
legs wild to go dancing and she knows
the Pontiac dealer wouldn't mind sliding
a finger or two up them. She is 29,
holding a baby; she doesn't know why it
took the man she eloped with, with suit-
cases of condoms, 3 months to take off
peach satin flapper panties that will press
themselves, at the end, up close to a box
of Depends. She is 24, in love with the
man she can't marry, no longer 11, fat
with frizzy hair in a town where every
body goes to a Christian church. She
vows if she ever has a daughter, swears
she'll never end up in this too pretty
New England town. She wants to travel,
dance on her toes. She loves the sound
of the subway. My mother is 15 in the
smallest bedroom in the house, late June
when even in Vermont heat stays in the house.
She is too young to imagine packing the
camisole she will buy for another to escape
what she knows she can't have as peonies
fill with ants under a new moon, red and white
spirea dripping and the yellow roses, her mother,
unable to sleep, in a tall bed alone, knows are

climbing the trellis my mother can barely see
but dreams she will have a daughter who, like
them, will be beautiful, hearty and prickly,
who she will name Rosalyn for them

☐ from another world

A week after my mother's real birthday

I think of my grandmother pushing
as the black hair billowed between
her legs. "A girl," the midwife
frowned, and my grandfather
walked out of the house
slowly. Nobody in Mineville
recorded the birth for three days.
No one told a relative, told my
grandmother about how
milk would come. "I did
not even know the way you
got babies," she'd tell her
baby's child. Waves of blood
stained the feather quilt brought
from Odessa and someone
burned it. She didn't think
of eating until the plum
sun was swallowed by Lake
Champlain ten hours later
and then asked for buttered
bread in milk, not too cold,
what she'd had and would have
for many years to come, in houses
on Elm Street and North Pleasant
and what her daughter, 79 years
later, would call for as she moaned
Mama her last afternoon

Cows, dolls and babies float in my mother's head like in a Chagall painting

under the pines
in the heat,
the cat howling,
my mother telling
how she remembers
their cat cried
all night when my
grandmother was
wringing her hands
in the ferns, her
sister dying at
24, the 5th baby
in her: my mother's
aunt Carrie who gave
my mother pennies
to buy what her
own children sold
on a table by the
road where a cow
had to be milked.
My mother said
she never got the
wishbone doll she
wanted or one
with a head after
her grandmother
ripped the face
from a grimy rag
carnival doll
because my mother's
mother was pregnant

and the baby might
look like that,
the last words
something in her
throat exploded
were *Frieda, I'll*
get you a new doll
the first time
I'm out of bed

She was Frieda Lazarowitz

That late-May morning she pushed thru
her mother's thighs, the first of four.
Maybe because the apple blossoms were
wildly white with sweet snow, they gave
her May for a middle name. Frieda May
Lazarowitz in the small New York town
of Mineville, where her father sold pots and
pans and she saw an egg filled with blackness.
When they packed, took the ferry over Lake
Champlain toward green mountains that
looked blue, a blue she would wish her eyes
were, she huddled on the deck against her
mother's blue afghan. Frieda May Lazarowitz
in the house on Elm St with a curtain of beads
sun went amber and raspberry thru until they
moved around the corner. Lazarowitz, a name
hard for a child to say, harder with her father's
Russian accent when he opened Middlebury
Supply Co, sure no one in town would be
able to say it. An apple tree bloomed in the
backyard. She could see yellow roses from her
small front-room window. Her father was
hearing more about these Model T Fords. He
buys the children barrels from the store they could
peel hoops off and play with. Frieda Lazarowitz,
the oldest, and a girl, enough to deal with without
having a kid brother smashing her dolls. Once when
she ran toward a doll's arm on the floor near the
stove, her grandmother came toward her with a
knife for its coldness but my mother just saw the
blade. Her father, uncertain what to do with a
girl but make her likeable, musical, got her a

violin. The violin teacher, with an even longer
Russian name, took Fredela Lazarowitz out of the
bright sun and made her practice scales that always
squeaked. She was Frieda Lazarowitz in the down-
stairs den with a fever on a small cot, her skin burning,
feeling her father squeeze into the bed with the hired girl
whispering, *pussy, pussy*. Nobody could say "Lazarowitz"
the first day of school. They were different, got meat
from another town. Corn grew in the backyard. Her
father had some of the first cars in town. No more horse
and buggy, no pack on his back but black enameled
Chinese chairs in the living room, etched glass, a bronze lady
with a light growing over her raised hand not unlike the
Statue of Liberty. My mother's mother joined clubs and had
the church ladies over for tea. Then, as suddenly as my
mother got a favorite dog and lost it—as fast as blood would, a
few years later, to her terror, appear in her panties—her father
brought home not another baby but a new name. Her violin
teacher screamed, *Now you will never become a famous violinist!
How can you do this, Harry?* My grandfather might
      have shrugged
and ignored him. He shaved just enough of the letters off
      so they
wouldn't forget where they came from. Not to Lake or Lane
but something with its own story. Now Frieda May Lazarowitz
became Frieda Lazarus. Maybe, though she would have liked a
more American name, she tried it out like new ice skates and
dreamed it meant that with everything that was about to unroll
and change, like with Lazarus, there'd be miracles to come

☐ the days between

June 30, 1938, record cold

My mother in the
small front room,
packing with the
door locked
as if to smuggle
cargo out past
peonies and
yellow roses in
to the car she
wouldn't know
until days later
had been borrowed
without the brother-in-
law's knowledge before
his 4th of July
vacation. Tiger
lilies and chicory,
blue and orange
tongues. She tears
up the letter from
the one her mouth
waters for; she knows
even then she can't
keep him but not that
she will never not long
for him. Crystal beads
on a string already
discoloring glitter
in the moon. She
packs beaded silk

she doesn't yet
know she'll have
little need of
like the condoms
she'll see spilling
from the suitcase
of the man she knows
if she waited to plan
a wedding with
instead of eloping
she wouldn't

The night before I was born

did my mother look
toward the moon
past the lilies,
one hand on her
belly, the other on
breasts that would
not stay inside the
bare midriff top?
Maybe my father
wanted to stop
for a beer at the
Brown Derby
and she said she
didn't think so,
made a cup of
coffee. Lily of the
valley on cotton
in a drawer. She
dabbed her wrist,
wanted to get on
with what she still
didn't know she'd
never be over with

July 12 birthday poem

How could I not think of my mother? Not the hottest
July, as it was the year she was born, but even in northern
Vermont, with no air conditioning, the hour's drive from
Barre in the old black Plymouth, which her father bought her
since my own father hadn't, must have been stifling.
The car swerved thru hills that would turn orange in
three months, the guard rails painted over from where

the last car slid thru. Maybe she took the small suitcase
she brought to college and later I took to camp with its
Simmons banners now full of beaded 20s flapper dresses
she would not, after I slid from her, wear again. On Tuesday
night maybe they ran out of the house to the Catholic hospital
where my mother vowed she'd have her first child when nuns
and priests saved her mother after a car tore my grandparents'

car in two and my grandmother was pronounced dead in the
Burlington paper but the nuns prayed in their way and brought
her Friday candles to light and when my grandmother recovered
my mother told them, in thanks, her first would be born there tho
later she swore she'd do it differently next time. Though she
never talked about it, I wonder if my mother felt the lack of the
curse was her curse? Feel nothing at first when she tried to

let milk come into my mouth with little luck? And was that
why she spent the rest of her life trying to feed me? And if she felt
nothing holding what she felt she should, is that why she spent
every last day of her life after that trying to convince us both
that I was the only thing from then on that truly mattered

On the fifth anniversary of the night she eloped

my mother lay twisting
under damp sheets, the
second daughter, a dark
tiny thing, a birthmark
like a scar. She worried
about the older daughter,
the one there was time
to have birth cards printed
for, pick a name that
sounded fit for an actress,
announces her "presentation"
and "continuous performance."
That first baby blurred any
regrets over the choice she
made, eloping thru dripping
roses. But this second
one, so far, nothing like her
name, *Gay*, howls by her
side, here too fast, as if
already plotting to disrupt
time tables, plans, to wriggle
wildly from anything that
might hold her

The bottle of teeth

baby teeth, dried blood
still on them. Sharp
still as certain phone
calls. None of them
crumbling. Labeled.
"Rosalyn's 1st lost
tooth, July or was it
September," kept like
diamonds or a flapper
dress studded with
crystal on silk that
falls apart at a touch.
Packed away just so
she could put her hand
on them, as she wanted
me to be. She saved
every letter since
second grade, old
jewels, touchstones,
hand-knit baby clothes,
triplicate news clips,
every mention of
my name as if they
were me

"Vamoose," I hear a 30s or 40s torch singer belt out

a word I haven't heard since
my mother giggled it
when we packed the
car on an afternoon my
uncle closed the store early
so we could escape to the
beach, splashing, even thru
the hall, as we grabbed
bathing suits and bathing
caps, her otters, wild
to plunge into jade ripples.
We packed our rubber
dolls with iced tea and
salmon croquettes, drove,
windows down on Rte 7,
our hair tangling, my
mother's black curls and
cigarette smoke swept
toward the black seat.
With light going raspberry,
she held our hands at
the edge, watched us
float into the green
skin of water that
held us as her eyes
did from the shore

In Rexall's, Middlebury

the dark booth held us like a cove.
My mother put on high heels and lipstick.
Fruit parfait in glasses, a sweetness.
A comfort to eavesdrop on the others talking.

My mother put on high heels and lipstick.
My father never cared if we had a real house
where my sister and I wouldn't be ashamed to bring friends.
In the dark of the booth, I could imagine, someday, being a beauty.

My father never cared if we had a real house.
My mother never wanted to come back to this town
she eloped to escape.
She went out with realtors for 15 years.
In her last weeks she said if she could go anywhere she would
pick New York City

My mother never wanted to come back to this town,
imagined the bustle of cities, the theater, the subway.
My father sat in the yellow chair, read the *Wall Street Journal*
without talking.
My mother played gipsy music and Cab Calloway, "Raisins
        and Almonds."

I imagined the bustle of cities
where what happened mattered.
My father sat in the yellow chair quiet as stones.
Bits of my mother's red lipstick swirled in fruit parfait.
The dark booth held us like a cove

The blue violin candy dish

only the top was left from.
I think of it on the Heywood-
Wakefield coffee table my
mother's Marlboro's left
small dusty ovals on. Blue
as my sister's eyes so I
was sure she was adopted,
mysterious as the inky
velvet couch, the pillows
worn and flat as my mother's
dream of a house where we
could bring boyfriends.
Blue glass, twisting the
grey Main Street light
to navy and teal, cobalt.
January afternoons, snow
dingy and stained. It was
piled with chocolate
for babysitters, red lip
color kisses New Year's
Eve. When I cleared out my
mother's apartment,
deep in the built-in china
closet, broken salt shakers,
torn books, pieces of
what would never go back
together and the cover
of the old dish. When I saw
the fragments, I wanted
to lug what couldn't
be fixed to my house but
the van was full. I threw the

pieces away. When I hear
someone has the bottom
of the dish that became
a catch-all for what didn't
have a place, I think of my
sister and me stealing candy
from the blue violin,
covering for each other,
how it is never easy to know
what not to keep

☐ interlude

My mother in front of the powder-flecked vanity

a bottle of Arpège in one
hand, silver mirror in the
other before she'd frown

into a magnifying mirror,
shake her head and
whisper, "I don't

like me." She smoothed
her black dress over
legs that would never

lose their lush
shape even when she
could hardly stand on

them. It's too early
to look back at years
she could bolt up

Beacon Street in 5-inch
heels, not doubting the
Red Sox would win

My mother's knife

Tonight she calls: she
remembers when it must
have happened, the year,
you know, she says, when
the trees slammed down.
That was when I started
missing. Remember they
came because their
roof had blown away?
It would have been
easy enough for her to
take something bigger,
all the people and no
lights. I've looked 19
years and couldn't find
a knife like that. It
makes me boil. When I
saw it in *her* kitchen
I should have said *Sally,*
that is mine but
she was saying how she
needed, couldn't get
along without that
knife, wherever it
came from. My mother
stops in Macy's knife
department each time
she comes, mourns the
gone steel, the perfect
dark brown handle.
She dreams this knife

is why Sally is a
little cold and doesn't
want anyone to just
drop by

Tho my mother said she forgot how to make hospital corners

she remembered the rules of Solitaire to
the end played on the blue velvet couch
waiting for my phone call, checking
the clock that in the last years in her
flat froze for months and then began
again. Checking for a flight or a
landing, she slapped down cards
instead of drinks or Librium, hearts
like my heart she was sure would be
broken by some man I'd chosen,
dumbly, a heart she wanted for her
self like those cards from the first deal
that could keep them going. The first
born, I was her queen, her diamond.
Tho she didn't drink, she collected sweet
wines in pastel bottles, odd-shaped glass
with bells and beads now sticking to the
wood in my upstate house. If she had
been a drinker she would have ended
most nights on the floor. Chocolate
was her heroin until, able to eat any-
thing and still stay slim, she couldn't.
Instead of a glass, she clutched the deck
of cards. Instead of a set-up of brandy or
bourbon she lay out the tableau of seven
columns—I can't quite remember the
object. This is what she did so nervously
and especially after she stopped lighting
up one Tareyton after another to get
thru the night, to wait for my voice.
Did she care about the odds of winning?

Or even what it meant to win? Trucks
rambled thru Main Street, dark as
Midnight Oil blues, the Rouge et
Noir and the Black Hole like scat she
used to dance in 4-inch spikes to the
black and red swirling in the shadows

I think of my mother on the blue couch

or maybe under the caramel
light at the dining-room table,
paper and pills that spilled from
the ruby punch bowl pushed
aside. My mother, with the
most phone calls in college,
now waits, anxious, for my
voice in the night, wants to
call me for the 11th time. She
will play one hand of Solitaire
to keep from reaching for the
dial, will deal the cards instead
of gulping a Librium. If my
mother drank she would have
climbed to the shelf of wines
and cordials in odd-shaped
bottles: fish, pineapple, cherries.
In college they begged my mother
to get her own phone so some-
one else could get a phone
call, wrote in her yearbook that
she had more boys, more people
laughing in her room. "You got me
thru the year—without you, I
couldn't make it," from a blonde
beauty who only knew how to get a
date one way. I think of my mother
daring someone to drive from Vermont
to New York City or Boston for a
cup of coffee, of how she knew every
one in her building the first week
in Manhattan. Then I see her in

dim light, the cards in her hand. She
didn't get the good cards, doesn't
really care about winning if it means
not having all the hearts she holds left

My mother begs me to wait with her in the dark

under the blood
red dogwood
berries, trillium
crinkly as skin.
My mother whose bed
I'd curl into the
whole year I was
six, woke up
dreaming of fire,
doesn't want to
be alone. Between
the car and the
house, shorter than
the hallway to her
blue room where
Otter Creek Falls
licked the window
she holds onto the
car like an old
doll, the Lindbergh
doll I smashed
in a tantrum. My
mother who'd take
subways at night
all thru Brooklyn
is afraid in the
driveway of Apple
Tree. *Don't leave
me* she cries like
a child begging
for water she'll
never drink

My mother, who could always see a smudge of grit on the scrubbed bathtub

is finding outlines blur,
the sweater on the chair
looks like the cat. "Memento?"
She calls toward the rolled
wool. My mother who always
could find things every-
body else lost, contact lenses
that slipped away 3 months
before she came, can't find
crackers she wants in
Grand Union, mistakes
curbs and stairs. I
remember my grandmother
curled under her rainbow
afghan, all peach and cherries,
tangerines, recognizing me
by my voice, whispering
"Lyn, is it Lyn?", her lip
like my mother's when
she dozes under the
velvet spread I snatched
on an iced night in Hudson,
frost on my bedroom
wall. She can't see I
may have on too much
eye liner, rouge
the cat's tongue on her
dish, salt stains
on wood that's no longer
polished as ice-rink
ice, that I'm not still 17

My mother's tub

is all she can deal
with and have as
she wants. The
house sticks its
tongue out at
her like some
vicious teenager.
Old televisions
fall from shelves,
threaten to crush
her. What spilled
on the 35-year-
old crackled kitchen
linoleum resists
ammonia and SOS.
Only the tub is
smooth, a newborn
who'll lie there,
be there. Or a
lover's arms, ready
to hold her, rinse
what no regrets
or letters could
from her, soothes
and lets her fill
and empty and take
care of like a baby
she could have a
second chance to
have turn out right

There's nobody

she says, who wanted
to dance more. *I'd
dance on the table,
Mike watched for
Gramp. I knew he
wouldn't like it.
The mahogany table,
I took off my shoes
as red spirea was
falling.* My mother,
with great turn-
out at 70, can stand
on her toes. The
man who loved her
at 18 says, "Look,
she's still got
great legs." *I'd
have done anything,
studied acting,* she
says, *Gramp with
his hand on every
hired girl's skin,
groaned, none of
his, not his girl.*
My mother, who can't
spring up from sitting
cross-legged
on the floor, who
used to dance to
balalaika strings
in the hot apartment
on Main Street

kicking her legs
up under gipsy
skirts, still wants
to learn some
Cossack squat
and kick steps

The leaves cold, thick

as damp ginger.
Red globes drip
from the dog-
wood, smear
red on slate. My
mother is sliding
from me like
that color in September
rain I can taste
already coming, try
to grab on to her,
ask does she want me
to hold on to her,
the stairs tilting.
She shakes, doesn't
know how, she says, she
can get thru another
snow, wants my
fingers, holds them
tighter, *want to,*
Honey, I never want
to let you go

After my mother goes

the clock ticks two days
in her bedroom like breath.
Batteries she bought me
in a drawer, as if she could
keep away the darkness.
Part of me wants to curl
into her arms, to dissolve,
a kitten embryo absorbed
into the mother cat's blood,
to escape. The tins of salmon
lugged home from Grand Union,
the tiny yellow clocks to
glue to dashboards and mirrors,
the envelopes of coupons
she clipped in the dusty
apartment on Main Street,
the strands of grey hair
on velvet pillows will
haunt like the yellow cat's
fur still in the scratched
brown burlap couch four
years after he died

☐ flickering light

My mother's last trip on her own to Grand Union

in pewter wind. Maybe
she thought if she could
get out and back it would
mean things were normal.
She took her fold-up cart, went
thru the park, uphill past
where my father fell in snow,
breaking his nose, a rose,
huge rose in the snow
blossoming. Four days
after the call from my sister
telling her to read about
toxic parents, she put on
one of the four hat scarves
she bought in Macy's after
losing one in the spring,
felt the wind but kept on
walking as if going thru the
Grand Union aisles would
make this day like any other,
a day ending in front of the
TV with a chocolate-swirl cake.
Maybe she'd find something she
felt like eating. Maybe she'd
see someone she still knew.
Only once there, she forgot
what she needed, felt so
tired she shook her
head calling for a cab, hoped

she wouldn't have to
wait for hours, scared, still
never supposing she
wouldn't do this

That April

my mother wanted to go back
to her rooms. "A hazard,"
my sister blurted, "the
clutter, the air." My
mother said she wanted
her cleaning woman to
come, wanted to cook me
lamb chops, well done, in
her new oven. "On IV," my
sister shrieked, "Mother
can't travel," but my
mother insisted she would,
wanted to doze on
the blue sofa a cat once
peed on. Maybe she wanted
to fall asleep for the last
time lulled by Otter Falls.
"Mama," I said, "let me show
you photographs of the
waterfalls in Hawaii,
long cascades, Bridal Falls."
"And do you think, Honey,
you'll marry again?" she
smiled and leaned back, her
eyes closed, slid her ring
onto my finger

My mother used to rub my back

told me if I couldn't
sleep any time of
the night to call
her in Vermont.
Or from the next room
she'd come
to soothe or
sing years after
I was a child,
bring me ice cream.
Now I'm sitting at
the foot of the
bed where she's
my baby, a child
who'll only
wither, baby of
snow, shrinking
faster in my
arms and hands
the closer I
hold her

My mother, just looking out at me

the TV on, her
back to it, gazing.
Her eyes for weeks
already different
as if looking some-
where I couldn't see.
I couldn't see myself
reflected in them,
even leaning close,
holding her until
she pushed me aside,
hating my hair on
her, hair she'd told
me was beautiful
before I ruined it.
"Do you want me
to cut it?" I hissed as
if "hair" was me

Red sky at morning

Later, I wouldn't need
a photograph to picture you

deep under lilies. That room
half underground, a rehearsal.

Your hair, a white river
flowing to join other rivers.

Asked a wish, you said
only to hear the diagnosis

was wrong

a marbled rose
on the pond,
thick mist like
mornings my mother's
hair seemed to be
sending out flares,
throwing life lines,
lush and thick
as it never was
taking on a new
shape in the
rooms half under-
ground as if
growing into the
last pillow to
comfort her

Your mother has too much fight to be anywhere near death

the IV nurses said but I knew
my mother for the actress she
was. Not just how she could sound
like she was mortally stabbed in
a ditch with her body burning if she
couldn't get me on the phone. Or
how, from Intensive Care when her
heart beat went crazy, she acted
calm as Bette Davis brushing off
a flea or a man. Her "Honey, I love
you" voice could move me to
feel nothing would not be perfect,
tho her "I know, now, how you
feel" made my gut twitch and burn.
Academy Award performances to
men I hardly knew made them sure
she was on the verge of whatever
part she chose for the moment. It
was New York City she loved,
Broadway, and the Music Tent on
the Cape. She filled the house with
comedy-and-tragedy plaques, lamps,
jewelry, ashtrays. I knew her masks,
knew it didn't mean much that she
acted so feisty, that it wasn't her but
a part she could peel off in hours when
she called the nurse *Vampire*, said *I
know you want to suck my blood* and
put her vomit tray up as a cross,
giggling and loving watching them laugh
the day before the curtain went down

That last afternoon my mother wanted bread and butter in milk

as if she was already
stepping back, moving
into a place she can't
take me with her. She
doesn't want my fingers
on her skin. It's the
first time she doesn't
want her back rubbed,
or touched, moving
back to the green
glider, ripped and
faded, past the
stained glass in the
hall and up where
wasps fell on their
backs. My mother
doesn't eat the bread
she wanted, her skin
marbling. I sat on the
grass that morning,
saw the leaves dying
as my mother was
almost tasting the
bread and butter her
mother would bring
out on the porch as
roses sucked on the
mango and amber
light before dark

My mother wants buttered bread in milk

Hours before, she asked for hot
chocolate, wanted me, not any
nurse. The day after fog gulped
branches and we watched films
all afternoon before chicken and
the strawberries I was still smashing
Demerol into. *Butter*, she said,
but thinly, you always do it too
thick, and she drifted back. The
nurse said this was it, whispered,
"Frieda, you're not in pain still,
are you, Honey?" and I, in my own
daze, repeating "I love you,"
cringed when my mother shook her
head, called "Murray, Mama, Lyn,"
the morphine, the last of only two
she'd have put in her, melting. "You
know I do" I said over and over,
the butter melting, a slick on the milk
as time was warped, telescoped.
Cars lined the lawn, women with
noodles saying to eat, that I had to.
Food slid down as sheets did from
my mother's leg, her foot twitching.
"She has no blood pressure," a nurse
said, bread and butter taking my
mother back maybe to the kitchen
table in the house under pines, always
cool near the pantry where there'd be
brownies or yellow cake or lemon
meringue, my mother calling for my

grandmother in that house in her mind,
in the front room where she could see
yellow roses and peonies poke thru,
where the cold pulls away from

Strange pocketbooks scattered thru the house

my mother's special one,
always full of bank books,
now in the closet near my
bed. She kept the bags
locked in a suitcase, kept
her wits, even two weeks
from dying so none of this
was left in the room where
my mother and I could
not stay. Kleenex still in a
ball in one bag, lipstick in
some other compartment.
The first time I saw it on
her bed with her not in the
house it was like a knife,
a warning. Now it's in a
separate closet, not where
I sleep, as if I would dream
her into the room, lugging
the glasses she always
thought she lost, asking
if I want ice cream or
to have her rub my back
and then wake up shaking
at what isn't. I keep the
black bag from my ex-mother-
in-law with my mother's
emerald, a gold chain to
suck spring colors into the
room like forsythia I
cut at the end of January,
starved for what could
still bloom in greyness

☐ returning in autumn

"You must have had an actress in the family"

the woman with black curls
beams at the garage sale,
her arms loaded with comedy-
and-tragedy plaques in gold
and licorice and the ashtray
with those masks on an edge.
Earrings of smiling and
weeping faces fall from her
fingers. "Can I pile what I
want here?" she begs. "Oh
you can see this family was
unique, eccentric, I already
love them." She grins, reaches
for my mother's black lace
gown and 5-inch heels that
caught the hem dancing
a cha cha near the piano in
the grey living room. The
woman's black curls shake
like my mother's as she steps
into black and gold mules and
says if I ever want to sell
the comedy-and-tragedy
lamp I've told her about or
the piano in the living room,
she'd buy it. I think of the
years in 38 Main Street over
Otter Creek, with raised,

projected voices, hysteria, how
the gut-bucket giggling had
filled rooms there never
wasn't drama in

It was all comedy and tragedy

even at the end. When my
mother quipped to the IV nurses
Oh, you vampires are here again,
never get enough blood, and the nurses
said, turning to me, "There's so
much fight in her left, no
way she's about to check out,"
I knew my mother for
the actress she was. Adept
at changing parts, her
voice could go from a bell to
a scream, depending on who
was at the other end of the
phone. She named me Rosalyn
Diane because it sounded like
someone in theater. Packing
up her rooms, drawers
spilled comedy-and-tragedy
pins, bracelets, earrings, dishes
in silver and copper. In the
storeroom closet, plaques in
black and gold: faces laughing
and crying. The comedy-and-
tragedy lamp seemed right
for the last room in my house
my mother slept in, denying
pain so well, we couldn't tell,
in control of her audience
to the end

Hearing "Bloomsday" as "Blues Day"

this week of rain,
the blues move in,
not something
blooming. Some-
one slashes the
roses. Crows and
gulls in the petals.
Geese my mother
would have walked
thru wet grass to
throw corn to, her
sneakers in a closet.
Before she died
she was in the bed
in the orange room.
Now she is
everywhere

Like a woman of ancient China

my mother wanted to take what
she cherished with her. Not jade,
not the emerald she mostly saw
as flawed, not statues or photo-
graphs of her mother: she wanted
to take *me*. If she could not phone
to see how I got home from a trip
or the mall, she could not rest.

"You're so thin," she said over
and over, "we could be buried
together in the same space." Though
she liked living alone as long as
she could phone me, eternity with-
out AT&T seemed scary. If I could
be close, as I was in the room "already

half underground," she grinned
over pills and IV, it might not be
so bad that she didn't get back to the
ocean and never got to Europe
or the West Coast to lie back with
her mouth full of dirt and never tell
the stories and secrets she meant to.

If she could still touch me

While I was looking for photographs

in the china closet
I had stripped and
sanded this grey
day with orchid
azaleas the only
color splashed on
the pewter I was
stunned by your
gold and white
dishes we ate
beans and barley
soup out of,
untouched as
long as you
have been

The emptiness, Nancy says

most everyone
has it. You can't
eat enough, hold
enough people
near you, can't
drink or take
enough pills,
have enough
lovers or babies.
Lyn, your mother
was so cold, she
was cold inside.
No one is warm
enough. She was
especially cold.
Your blankets,
your arms, every
thing you could
give her just
touched snow

Seeing the mother and daughter laughing over coffee in Macy's

it doesn't sting
as it might have but
sucks me back to
those mornings when
no one was mad and
you and I would
stroll thru the mall
as if we had
forever, dawdle
over barrettes you
wanted to buy me,
or demitasse cups,
thick towels on sale,
and if I didn't have
to rush back to ballet
or some man you'd
begun to resent
my seeing, we'd drive
out to some new
restaurant you had
a coupon for, buy
Halloween candy
and drive back near
midnight, the cat
waiting, and we'd
curl up on my bed
with chocolate or ice
cream, the doors
double-locked as if
anything threatening
could be kept out

Even after 9 years

the cards and stories I look
away from singe. On Mother's
Day everyone used to wear
carnations, red or pink if your
mother was living, white
if you were alone. I still
wear her sox, as if to keep
her reminding me what to
lock and what to open.
Every TV channel reels with
news of mothers and children
reunited after shootings,
tornados, exportations,
their fingers digging into each
other's backs, holding on to
each other the way people claw
rock when they lose their footing,
faces buried in skin and hair
so it's hard to tell where
one stops and the other starts,
Siamese twins in the night.
If my mother had held me
under a bridge during a
tornado, she couldn't have
let go, let the wind fling her
from me or see me swept
in the air to a tree where a
rescuer could find me. Our
bodies would have been
glued together and only
a force strong enough
to kill us both could
separate us

After the IV, after the Demerol and Compazine

after the beet juice, the bed pan,
after the back rub. After I combed
her hair and she smiled. After the
nurse's aide came in, the high of my
day, fresh coffee, June leaves
opening, light filtering thru. Just to
sit still, another night over, the air
still clear. Now, ten years later, my
cat, older in cat years than my mother,
comes back from *her* IV at the vet.
Pills in the bedroom. She too is
on hold, held on to, has such a hold
on this June, the same date my
mother came back from the hospital,
tethered, tied, a braid of need that
wouldn't loosen until it was cut. I
think of how I found needle caps for
years around my house later. Now I
turn the insulin carefully, re-read
instructions, uneasy as I was with my
mother suddenly in my arms, sliding
to the floor after a 7-hour trip from
Stowe mountains, when the IV team
left boxes of tubes, needles, syringes,
and said: "Read the instructions." First
the cat pulls away but then I get her,
put a needle in, pull the plunger. There
can never be bubbles. I remember that,
check for nothing wet or leaking as I
would my mother's catheter. The cat
leaps off the bed toward food. It's
good to see her eating again and I go

down and grind caramel coffee beans,
a small break before the morning dash,
the moment to watch the roses unfold,
the only green there was that other June

Three days before my mother's real birthday

I think of the young woman I ran into last night
almost staggering across the street. I rarely see
any acquaintances in this town where people live
out of suitcases, so I'm surprised it's someone I
know. She seems pale. Then I see she's lugging a
cat case and when I ask if the cat is OK, she says
no, a tumor. 17 years old. I think of my own cat,
as old, how she has been drinking so much water,
of how this year's been a gift after the vet said
a year ago she was dying. A reprieve, an extra 4
seasons. I think how, when she doesn't eat, I'm
afraid, how it reminds me of my mother those last
months, when I shopped wildly for treats, something
that might tempt her as chocolate no longer could. I
bought her Popsicles in exotic flavors—blueberry,
mango, apricot—but still she kept shrinking until
we no longer weighed her. All winter, coaxed and
spoiled, my cat thrived, too heavy to jump up on
the bed, clawing her way in the night and nibbling
dry food. Now with the air conditioning on, she
chooses a chair where it's warm, some days seems
to be slipping from me as my mother did when she
stopped worrying when I drove from the mountains
to my house or caring what I ate or where. On her good
days, my mother and I sat in the jade light outdoors
and I brought her watermelon or strawberries and
cream, one of the few things she still longed for.
Today I opened extra cans for my cat and she nibbled
but she feels lighter. When I brought my mother to my
house, I knew what the end of her visit would be but

not how we'd get there, and I wanted to feel each day,
however it went, was a gift, wanted to feel grateful but
those last weeks, shriveling, she was like a kite I'd lost
the string to, getting smaller and smaller

May 28th, what would have been my mother's 90th birthday

once covered with stars, the
white petals just stud the edge
of the dogwood. On the day
she was born, record-breaking
heat: 97° in 1911. Here, it's
raw and grey. I'm in my New
York house, first time in half
a year. Her pocketbook in
the closet as if any moment
she'd come back, ready to
take off for Macy's. All
yesterday I swept: webs
and the wings of dead
insects, dried-up wings.
One morning I tried to reach
my mother thru the Morse
code of words on the page
but the only answer: squirrels
skittering across the room
and my 20-year-old cat
moaning in her sleep, maybe
dreaming she could leap
up to drink from faucets
whose water is cold as
underground springs

☐ things behind the sun

The wallpaper in my mother's hall

grey background with dark
rose figures floating on boats.
Maybe my mother saw them
as a way out, a slow boat to
anywhere but this calendar
town she grew up in and fled,
intoxicated by New York City,
Boston, Baltimore. *Trees,
scenery*, she'd scowl, wanting
theaters, French restaurants,
a boat ride on the Charles, some
one to go with her to lectures
and plays. Deep in the storeroom
closet she never got to sort out
rolls of the wallpaper, brittle and
fragile as the life she didn't lead
for long. In her last days, asked
where, if she could go anywhere,
she would choose, her eyes lit up,
New York. She took us to plays,
to Greenwich Village where
Theodore Bikel was playing in
the square. *Honey, the city is so
magical*, she grinned, and now on
trips from Virginia to upstate New
York, I only want to be awake for
the lights from the Empire State
Building and the Chrysler Building,
city rhinestones and diamonds, as
much her as this wallpaper she never

changed from the 40s, hanging in
strips now, like her skin did when she
was no longer plump and strong and
able to open jars nobody else could.
I imagine leaning against the warm
marble topped radiators, my mother
talking to a friend as Otter Creek
roared and the traffic sloshed thru
December. Snow on Main Street, the
jasmine leaves in a young Asian woman's
hair, a pale rose I wanted to be thin
enough to look as fragile in

Feet

Not allowed to take ballet,
her father—lecher and gawker
at nuns and babies—said it
was not moral until, dying,
he apologized, said he was
wrong. My mother danced
on a table with the door
locked, could stand on her
toes barefoot, and tho she
married a man who would
never try to tango, before
then, before fun ended, she
had to be dragged off the
dance floor. At 70, she
could bolt up Beacon Hill,
outwalk me in malls. No
"old lady" shoes for her
(until the last weeks) but four-
inch spikes or five. In her
closet, shoes from years
of dance tho it had been
ages since she was the girl
with the most phone calls
in college, ready to drive to
New York City for a cup
of coffee, but the shoes,
silver, gold, patent leather
sandals, wait patiently
in the talcum dust for her
to be ready for them again

The gold dress

The threads glisten almost
like a night light, untouched,
not worn for years: my
mother's dress for the
wedding, in photographs
in a film my sister hoards so
you can't see my mother's
arms move toward me,
how the bright petals were
less bright than her eyes.
The dress waits, encrusted
as moss on a stone. Sequins
would have lost their color
by now, like her bones. If I
put it on, it might scorch like
an icy railing on the tongue. For
one day only, it held my mother
like a vase and she bloomed
like the lilacs in the myth of
the apartment a gone lover
filled with orchid, lavender,
violet and snow boughs.
When it held her, it held her
as close as a lover, didn't
suffocate but let her move
and dance, hold me in the
mirror. Never something I
would or could wear, I
brought it to my house to
hang like a totem of what's gone,
the print a leaf makes in stone

or amber. The dress takes a
deep breath, waits patiently
for something that filled it
to fill it again

Wintergreen

always there in my mother's
pocketbook between eye-
glasses, a broken watch,
coupons, lipsticks, keys
she was always sure she'd
lost. In her last days, she
wanted the Life Savers on
the nightstand. Like Joy
perfume and Jolie Madame,
a whiff of wintergreen is
the smell of my mother,
what she longed for her
last years as she had longed
for emeralds, for green to
move into late Vermont
winter snow. When I saw
a field of it, smelled the mint,
I wanted to scoop it up and
bring it to her. Wintergreen
in silver foil, clean and fresh
as a night the stars are silver
fish, the moon a silver apple.
When we drove past Silver
Moon Diner or cranberry
bogs she always asked if I'd
like a mint, gave me the roll
smelling faintly of her lilac-
scented lipstick and, for years,
of Marlboros and Tareytons,
the sweetness melting as cities
did behind us, comforted like
air, the first day of snow when
nothing is stained or walked on

In my mother's wooden medicine cabinet

lightly coated with powder, thin vials
of cologne designed to smell like
other scents. Twist and break the glass:
forest blends or flowers or spice,
fragile as the blown-glass giraffe whose
snapped neck once oozed sweetness,
probably there since WW2. One
package has each vial tipped with a
different color, orange or green,
cobalt, wine, pewter, gold, pink, sun
yellow. Each has a name: Consent,
Secret de Suzanne, Yram, Repartee,
Devastating White Lilac, Conflict,
Shining Hour, Tweed, Escapade,
Midnight, Blue Carnation, Jealousy,
Black Satin, Evening in Paris, Fleur
d'Amour, Shining White Mist,
Strategy, 4th Dimension, Silver Night,
Breathless, Tapestry. I think of my
mother, younger that I am now,
watching Otter Falls on a night she
couldn't sleep, wondering if her babies
were safe from Hitler, wondering if
the man she didn't marry would find
her devastating and breathless still, and
if, in this small town she never wanted
to come back to, anything would seem
like a shining hour on a silver night
of escapade

The guava and turquoise bath mat

My mother probably chose
the color of the bathroom
paint around it. A wedding
gift circa the late 1930s.
Not stuffed away but on
the bathroom door of the
one room you could be
safely locked away in.
Used every day, except
when it was in the wash.
It could have just come
out of a gift box, the
colors so bright, the
cotton thick and warm.
Even the bath mat shows
only a little wear. It if
could talk, what stories
of the feet it hugged, the
toes trembling and scared,
or wild to leap into arms
that dance them around
until where they stood
blurred

The red sweater

The skating sweater,
she called it. I mostly
shivered and stumbled
on the wrong kind of
blades in the rink behind
the grade school. Itchy,
not my favorite color,
the sweater choked
my neck. I was sure
it smelled of whatever
sheep it was sliced from.
Like other rarely worn
clothes it hung in my
father's closet even while
he was still around. My
mother stopped wearing
turtle necks, hating to
be more suffocated than
she was, coming back to
her home town. I wish I'd
asked if my mother had
it in college, if she chose
the red. After the garage
sale I packed it up for the
woman who does costumes,
marveled that like so little
here it's without a hole.
Two days later, reboxing
photos, my mother is still
wearing it, pressing me to
those still bright threads,

me, 1 year 2 months, my
mother smiling, her teeth
perfect, showing off every
thing that mattered to her

My mother's nicotine-stained clock

round as an Art Deco
mirror, a Heywood-
Wakefield vanity's
curve, flowers of smoke
in the dial. If it moved,
a burst of Marlboro
or Herbert Tareyton
cigarettes would unravel
in Virginia, ten hours
away from where it
soaked up smoke and
dust 40 years. The cool
marble burns memories
into skin. If I licked the
glass I'd taste my mother

The mourning ribbons in boxes of jewelry

crushed in a tangle
of pearls and cameos,
the black smelling of

her cologne and
old lace huddled
in the plum velvet

like old men under
an eave in rain,
their night cloth

sleek but crumpled,
each wing cut,
wounded blackbirds

☐ darkness in the light

September 26, 1996

this morning the pond
looks like marble. Rose
and charcoal dissolving
to dove, to guava, rouge.
Only mallards pushing
holes in the glass, so
unlike the pond, deep in
trees, almost camouflaged,
startling as coming upon
your reflection in a mirror,
just there under trees and
the wooden bar and the
driftwood benches blackly
jade with pines dripping
into it, shadows close to
my hair. What I didn't have
blinded me so I hardly saw
the small birds, blue,
pulling out of moss and
needles as if reaching into
the dark for their color

Mid November

when the black ducks come,
winter opens, a kick pleat in darkness,

eyelash fringe of ferns on shore.
Late fall thunder after a long
Indian summer.

Branches creak. Muskrats slither into
the pond like a stone the tide covers
in the glow of a stranger's flashlight

Late November

Today in Virginia, unseasonably cold,
highs only in the mid 30s.
I think of a night drive from Austerlitz,
an hour north, to bring in my plants, early September.
The sky tangerine, guava and teal.
My own house strangely quiet, my
cat at my mother's.

When I think of a night I drove from Austerlitz
to bring in the plants, my mother young enough
to swoop up suitcases, my cat,
I was looking for someone. "Aren't you glad you
still have me?" my mother purred. The cat I
got after that one, now going on 21,
the ice yesterday a warning.

I was looking for someone. Each time I
left my mother's rooms, drove thru
Vermont leaves there was an ache becoming myself.
When the wind tore thru yesterday, on the stairs, a
shape that looked like lint with claws.
Later I tucked the geraniums in quilts
As if putting a child under flannel or leaves.

That ache, a wind under my hair.

My mother tucked in the earth.
The headless fur shape with its pink claws
or feet, on its back, a mystery.
Today in Virginia, unseasonably cold

Just after forsythia, after icy rain

Rattlesnake Mountain
pokes up thru the clouds
and we drive past pastures
and tangled orchards.
Trees squeak, green fur
in the wind sounds like
dolphins calling. Above
a field of trillium, the
Liz Taylor of wildflowers,
a nipple hill of snow
dotted with mayapple
and bloodroot. Indians
used it for war paint.
Wintergreen we pick for
tea. Deerberries and
yellow lady's slippers. In
this quilt of pastels, I
think of what the blind
would smell, the musky
damp wood, the earth
opening. I think of those
on the island where no
one sees in color seeing
70 shades of grey in
the leaves and as the
light goes, the glint and
shimmer, the texture of
petals in near darkness

When spring melts the ground

the dead start stretching,
wonder what's next. All
winter in quilts of white,
colorless as their wrists
and bones are becoming.
They think they ought to
be hungry, ought to feel
around for photographs
of the ones who followed
them to this dark bed and
then turned their backs.
The dead wonder if this
is a bad dream, one in
which their old clothes
are lugged off in boxes and
their names crossed out of
address books, darkened
over with ink as if someone
were putting stones on their
coffins or weighting their
bodies before throwing them
overboard. When they feel
light move into the grass,
they remember lilacs,
white roots or trillium
like upside-down trees
in a negative. It's too late
to change things. Some-
times they smell fresh
flowers left on their grave

and feel less alone. It does
not hurt to know somebody
kneeling in wet grass
is as lonely

Days the dead are too loud

it could be, passing
Arlington Cemetery,
where the one I should
have flicked off me
like a moth or one of those
dark ants that drop
on the quilt from
varnished cherry
clanks bone under his
last bed. Green this
spring instead of blue
sheets are often in
rain. The world from
the metro, splashed
water, something
slippery, as light
flops up against a
fish soon in a different
world, still, beginning
to rot. Later I dream
the dead into my
kitchen with only
the sound of my cat
on tile, these
words like
strangers in the
distance on a ship
that's sucked down,
trying to tell you
what it's like
before it happens

Overnight the trees

leafed out, electric
chartreuse against
the charcoal sky.
More shades of green
than there seem
to be words for.
Something like a
huge black rose
is unfolding, as
unstoppable as the
sap rising in the
maples. A black
gauze. I think of my
mother's last spring.
The night moth of
sadness closes its
wings around cherry
boughs and all I
see are the holes,
what will only be
filled like graves with
what I can't keep

March 20, 2000

After weeks in the
80s, after cherry
boughs explode in
pale rose two weeks
early, the almost-
white white against
a milk sky. After
shivering past
people in parkas
trying to eat lunch
under the gnarled
bank or holding
three dogs in
blankets or in
hoods, the wind
kicking up, colder
than on New
Year's Eve Day.
After the cat coils
into her cloth
snake, her muff
on the bed and I'm
shivering in three
sweatshirts, I
turn the heat up,
chartreuse creeping
in slower these
last icy days,
stalling like a
woman who was
wild to open
suddenly pulling

her legs together,
the daffodils going
into fists, a cold
front, a hush of
ice. The pear
branches snow
could be snow

April

Yes, the loveliest,
a smudge of rouge
lips blotted against
dark boughs. Only
the pear and magnolia
ahead of the cherries'
blush lace, almost
a haze, almost a no
blossom snow any
storm could send
swirling, so by the
morning the lake
would have a skin
of rose, the trees
bare with just a fuzz
of green shaking

Some afternoons

like being in a rain forest
a green canopy over us,
whole roads in the sky.
Tons of other life floating
above us. No light filtering
thru except the green of
our bodies. No stars or
moon. Only what's half
made of the tent of our
skin, the damp inside a
mouth, thighs slippery as
everything ahead

Suddenly by the first of April, the palest rose wrapped tight

starts to bulge
overnight. Faint
chartreuse edges
out of color-
less branches,
the azaleas
exploding like
the first time
I saw what
nuzzled me on
the couch with
the lights off,
the first boy
in darkness,
suddenly glistening,
huge, pink, alive

In the park, before ballet

a man asleep on the bench,
head covered with a CVS bag,
a couple with braided arms
giggling past him, past the rose
of Sharon. An empty orange-
juice carton. Newspaper in
case of rain. Two years ago,
walking across this park,
pear blossoms exploding on
all sides, I thought of someone
who would always be missing.
New buildings instead of
trees. My old cat who slouched
all Sunday at the bottom
of the bed, her emerald eyes
glazed, her body a flung
glove, today asks for food,
as much a gift as this sun
must feel to the man
after weeks of rain, his
arms touching earth as if
waiting for a hand to
pull him back down

Quiet morning, August

after a night
floating from
the black river,
the moon clots
in feathers on
its skin, before
the geese and the
heat that bleaches
white from wood,
honey clots on
the counter,
smells of clover
and a trail
of sweetness
like Gretel left
in trees or long
strands of hair
pasted into an
envelope to a
stranger for
him to follow

Cherry blossoms in darkness

glow like
stars of lace,
heavy snow
clotting on boughs.
I couldn't sleep,
the sweet white
floating up-
stairs pulled me
back to the
cove of an
old lover's
arms, deep in
such white
dripping branches,
white petals
on slopes of
skin, lips
studding Tuesday
with jewels
in the sweet
grass, locked
like antlers

Downstairs, the dark studded

with glow of
white branches,
clots of snow,
stars in clumps,
you have to bury
your face in
white. In
Syracuse, off
Comstock, the
lilacs just
starting, the
first man who
touched me
inside my
clothes pulled
me under such
white boughs
thru rain dripping.
Lacy boughs, light
filling the
dark orchard.
In this same
jeweled light
everything
opening like
these clenched buds

☐ the wind won't carry us

The swans must be here

on the other side of the blinds
on the black glass of the pond.
I won't see them. They dissolve
in the light like those guava
streaks of carp, a slash of salmon
grosgrain, the kind of sun you
can't hold on to. Enough to know
they will leave a feather, other
clues. Even the geese are scarce
this April. The swans are still,
tho only some are mute swans.
They stay in the dark leaves
close to the water. The bed is
like a boat navigating by stars,
oblivious, like the birds, to the
squeal of the metro, cars. Some
times I'm sure I can hear the swans
breathe. Cattails and lilies graze
their beaks like mermaid's hair,
like my hair if I plunged in. At
night I imagine swimming close to
them, my pale hair like kelp, my
skin as colorless as the oval of their
bodies. Their black eyes are the
onyx my mother left me I could see
myself in, see her eyes as the river
currents rock us

Heron on ice

Pale salmon light,
9 degrees. Floor
tiles icy. Past
branches the
beaver's gnawed,

at the small hole
the heron waits,
deep in the water.
Sky goes apricot,
tangerine, rose.

Suddenly, a dive,
then the heron
with sun squirming
in his mouth, a
carp that looks a

third as big as he
is, gulped then
swallowed, orange
glittering wildly
like a flag or the

wave of someone
drowning

Dead goose the leaves drift over

still there when I come
back in wild rain, wind
blowing leaves against
where trees have shoved
it, camouflaging the
wound where the head
was. I think of the dead
mole on the art-colony
path, on its back, pale
belly, feet in the air,
almost human. At 1:30
I heard goose music
from the pond, slow and
deep as a cello in a minor
blue key, music for a
plane crash, mournful
as the stunned family
numb from the news, the
plane ride over the Nile,
Timbuktu, moonless,
starless, dark as the
streak of onyx feathers
glaring thru flame leaves

Dead goose under burnt orange leaves

after the rain
slammed sideways,
after lights went out
and the other geese
made a bracelet of
themselves until a
streak of salmon light
broke thru and the
pale heat lured them
toward the acorns,
across the green strip
over the body of the
bird gone stone

The mourning doves

For a week they
shuffle twig after
stick, pulling a bit of
twine into the hanging
purple fuchsia, cling to
the plastic edge
weaving pale branches.
There seems no
place to stand. The
birds beat their wings
balancing on the edge,
hovering like pale
hummingbirds while
frantically trying to
place the twig in the
right spot, make some-
thing perfect as a
Shaker chair. Their
cool olive-grey coats
punctuated by iridescent
guava, solid black
smoldering eyes. The
male dove watches
by day, on the roof
of the deck. Neither leaves
the nest. Pale white eggs
the size of Milk Duds.
I could lie on the deck
and watch the mother
in the deep petals,
her eyes like a doe's. Then,
she wasn't there. The

purple leaves, a
camouflage for the eggs.
It must have been a
crow, perching on the
fence, watching, swooping.
Even in the wild rain the
dove hadn't moved, was
deep in the flowers. It
must have been those dark
wings, the dove pulling
into herself, closer over the
eggs. She might have
already felt hearts beating,
the eggs already moving.
And then, nothing. In myth,
the crow is a bearer of bad
news, misfortune, a messenger
of death. It feeds on carrion,
a marauder, pillager, flying
black spike. A dove carcass,
someone says, near the pines,
half the pond away. The
crow, a splash of cold water ·

Swan-free, that's our goal, the warden says

Yes, I know they're exotic,
and we've pumped ourselves
up on myths of their charm,
but listen, they're dangerous,
aggressive, they take over,
take what belongs to those
that were here first. The
swans are outsiders, not
native, they're too pushy.
The birds make the lake
into squalor, the warden
says, they are predators.
We wanted to transport them
to Texas but we couldn't
round them up. They are
sneaky, they're smart. A
woman from Finland says
she was horrified: "Those
beautiful birds, I waited for
them each morning. I was
close enough to hear their
wings like breath. I never
thought a little town in Vermont
would remind me of the war.
They seemed connected
to myths in my past." We
did our duty, the men with
guns said, our orders. The
lake now is swan-free

LYN LIFSHIN is the author of more than a hundred books and chapbooks, including the major collections *Cold Comfort: Selected Poems 1970–1996* and *Before It's Light: New Poems*, both published by Black Sparrow. Her work has appeared in scores of American periodicals and has been included in many major anthologies of writing by women. She has given more than seven hundred readings across the U.S. and has appeared at Dartmouth and Skidmore colleges, Cornell University, the Folger Shakespeare Library, the Whitney Museum, and the Huntington Library. She has also taught poetry and prose writing at universities, colleges, and high schools, and has been Poet in Residence at the University of Rochester, Antioch College, and Colorado Mountain College. She is the recipient of numerous prizes for her work, including the Jack Kerouac Award, the Paterson Poetry Prize, and the Texas Review Award, and is the editor of four anthologies of women's writings, including the best-selling *Tangled Vines: A Collection of Mother and Daughter Poems*. She lives in Virginia and in upstate New York, and can be visited online at *www.lynlifshin.com*.

DESIGN & COMPOSITION BY CARL W. SCARBROUGH